Uncensored Hollywood

John Boldman

Contents

TALES FROM NEW HOLLYWOOD

Kathleen Turner said that when she became famous (and a sex symbol) through the film Body Heat, she discovered that a number of famous actors in Hollywood had a wager on who would sleep with her first. Turner made sure that none of them won the bet. Turner said the worst person she ever worked with was Burt Reynolds. She said Reynolds was a sexist bully who liked to be in charge of the set. As for the strangest person she ever worked with, Turner named Anthony Perkins. She said that before each take Perkins would sniff a mysterious drug and suddenly take on a wild eyed crazed appearance.

Eddie Murphy had an embarrassing time in the mid-nineties when he was caught in a red light district notorious for transsexual prostitutes. Murphy claimed that he had been out for a drive and stopped to help someone who seemed to be in trouble - who, to his great surprise, turned out to be a transsexual prostitute. It's safe to say that Murphy's claim of innocence was taken with a rather large grain of salt. After the story hit the headlines, a number of transsexual prostitutes came forward to say that Murphy was a regular visitor to the red light district and had sex with most of them. This was a PR disaster for Murphy because he'd recently refloated his flagging career by making a move into family films. To quash the scandal, Murphy's lawyer allegedly employed a Hollywood 'hustler' to bribe the prostitutes into changing their stories.

Hugh Grant was arrested in Los Angeles in 1994 after police officers saw a prostitute named Divine Brown (Estella Marie Thompson) get into his car. The police officers said that Grant was engaged in 'lewd' conduct with Brown when he was arrested. This was a highly embarrassing incident for Grant because he was in Los Angeles to promote his new film New Months. In what must have been an excruciating experience for Grant, he had to complete press obligations and appear on chat shows after his arrest. He was fined $1,180 and had to attend an offender education course on AIDS. Divine Brown made the most of her brief window of fame and appeared in porn films and radio interviews. She is said to have made over a million dollars. Though very embarrassing at the time, the incident had no great effect on Grant's career and was forgotten fairly quickly.

It is said that Jack Nicholson's cocaine habit was so out of control by the time he made The Shining for Stanley Kubrick that his drugs were part of the production budget. There was simply no way he would get through the film without them. In an interview at the time, Nicholson said that on average he spent about four days a week completely high. Dennis Quaid has also said that cocaine was allowed on the set of some early films he worked on and included in the budget.

Heidi Fleiss became infamous for being Hollywood's best known brothel keeper. Fleiss was tight-lipped on her clients but the usual suspects (Charlie Sheen) have been mentioned and Fleiss later had an obstreperous affair with the actor Tom Sizemore - who was arrested for making threatening phone calls to her and generally being aggressive and drug addled. It is alleged that George Lucas and Johnny Depp were among the names in the 'little black book' of Fleiss clients. Fleiss was given seven years in prison in 1994 for tax evasion but got a fresh wave of fame in 1995 when Nick Broomfield made a documentary film about her. These days, Fleiss runs a bird sanctuary and lives out of the limelight.

Jenny McCarthy said that when she auditioned for a part in the film Under Siege 2: Dark Territory, Steven Seagal asked her to remove her dress and do a nude scene. McCarthy decided to leave there and then. Portia de Rossi is another actress who found auditioning for Steven Seagal to be a creepy experience. "My final audition for a Steven Seagal movie took place in his office. He told me how important it was to have chemistry off-screen as he sat me down and unzipped his leather pants. I ran out and called my agent."

Julianna Margulies said she fled from an audition with Steven Seagal when she was 23. Margulies said that when she turned up for her audition, alarm bells began to ring when she deduced that Seagal was the only person there.

Little House on the Prairie star Melissa Gilbert said that when she auditioned to be in the Oliver Stone film The Doors in the early 1990s, she fled the audition in tears after Stone wrote a humiliating sex scene for her to play as part of the audition. Gilbert accused Stone of sexual misconduct and said he was exploiting actresses as part of the audition process. The part that Gilbert was auditioning for went to Meg Ryan in the end. On the production of the 2003 film Born Killers, Tom Sizemore was accused of inappropriately touching an eleven year-old child actress on the set. Sizemore was dropped from the film and dumped by his management company. The family of the girl did not press charges though and Sizemore, believe it or not, actually returned to do some reshoots.

Oscarexia is a term for how Hollywood actresses have to literally starve themselves before the Oscars so they can get into the slinky or revealing dresses they plan to wear. This would probably explain why, after she won an Oscar for Million Dollar Baby, a ravenous Hilary Swank was seen on Oscar night in a branch of Astro Burger wolfing down a vegetarian burger and fries as if she hadn't eaten for weeks.

Asia Argento was one of the first actresses to be vocal in regard to the sexual abuse that the disgraced Harvey Weinstein was responsible for. Argento said she was raped by Weinstein when she was 21. However, Argento got caught up in her own scandal when it came to light that she paid former child actor Jimmy Bennett $380,000 to try and stop him accusing her of sexual misconduct. Bennett was 17 and below the age of consent in California when he alleges that Argento gave him alcohol and had sex with him. What made the alleged relationship extra weird was that Bennett had previously appeared in a film with Argento as her son when he was seven years old. Bennett said he decided to speak out because he felt that Argento was a hypocrite for casting herself as a leader of the MeToo movement.

A man named John Rutter did a topless photo shoot with Cameron Diaz when she was a nineteen year-old aspiring model. In 2003, he approached Diaz (who was by now of course a Hollywood star) and told her that if she wanted the topless photographs to remain private she would have to pay him $3.5 million. Diaz refused to hand over the money and sued him for attempted blackmail. She had the last laugh when Rutter was sent to prison.

Jeffrey Jones is a familiar face on the big screen. He has appeared in films like Ferris Bueller's Day Off, Amadeus, Sleepy Hollow, The Hunt for Red October, and Beetlejuice.

In 2002 he was arrested for taking nude photographs of a teenage boy and also for possession of child pornography. The boy was 14 when Jones first photographed him. The punishment was five years' probation and counseling. Jones also became a registered sex offender. When he tried to return to work on the 2007 film Who's Your Caddy?, local people in South Carolina where the film was shot complained that the status of Jones as a sex offender was not communicated to the families who visited the set.

Brat Packer Rob Lowe was one of the first stars to suffer the indignity of a sex tape floating around. There were actually two Rob Lowe sex tapes in the late eighties. Lowe picked up two young women at a Democratic convention and then filmed himself having sex with them. The big problem for Lowe was that one of the women turned out to be underage. A second sex tape featuring Lowe and a young woman named Jennifer also surfaced. While he might have feared for his career, Lowe emerged from the sex tape infamy surprisingly well and avoided serious charges. The scandal was forgotten fairly quickly and Lowe was self-deprecating (and media savvy) enough to lampoon himself on television. One of the advantages for Lowe was that his sex tapes emerged at a time before the internet and so were seen by relatively few people.

In 1982, the Golden Globes gave the New Star of The Year award to Pia Zadora for her role in Butterfly. Zadora beat Kathleen Turner (Body Heat) and Elizabeth McGovern (Ragtime) to win this award. The decision baffled just about everyone. Zadora was a notoriously terrible actress and Butterfly had been completely panned. Zadora's surprise win made no sense whatsoever. No one had the faintest idea how she got nominated let alone won. The answer to this perplexing mystery soon became evident when it transpired that Zadora's husband, a billionaire named Meshulam Riklis, had flown members of the Hollywood Foreign Press Association to Las Vegas for a vacation and a meeting with Pia Zadora. Riklis had basically bribed and manipulated the press into giving Pia Zadora the award. Zadora's bizarre win was such an embarrassment that the Golden Globes scrapped the New Star of The Year award.

James Woods had an affair with Sean Young when they made the 1988 drama film The Boost. After the affair ended, Woods had to take out a restraining order on Young when he alleged she kept harassing him. Young even sent photographs of corpses and a disfigured doll to the home of Woods. Young claimed that Woods took out the restraining order because of spite that she had rejected him and that his claims were not true. The end result of the rumpus was that producers knew it wasn't a very good idea to cast Woods and Young in the same film again!

Steven Spielberg is famously mild mannered but one person who did visibly irritate him was Julia Roberts when she starred in his Peter Pan film Hook. At the time, Roberts had just cancelled her wedding to Kiefer Sutherland and moved in with Sutherland's best friend Jason Patric. It would be fair to say that Roberts was rather frazzled by all the turmoil in her private life. Roberts kept turning up to the set of Hook late and at one point irritated Spielberg no end when she called Action! (which is for the director to say - NOT the actor) on a take before he was ready. When he did a television interview for Hook, a brutally honest Spielberg simply said "no" when asked if he would like to work with Julia Roberts again.

Another person who made Spielberg angry was Megan Fox. Fox was one of the stars of the Transformers films that Spielberg produced for director Michael Bay. But when Fox, who is clearly neither a diplomat nor a rocket scientist, somehow contrived to liken Michael Bay to Hitler in an interview, an infuriated Spielberg had Fox immediately axed from the Transformers franchise. The loss of Megan Fox was not something that the Transformers crew shed too many tears over. It was reported that Fox was secretly mocked on the Transformers set for her limited 'porn star' acting range.

In 1987, Marlee Matlin won an Oscar for Best actress. She was the first deaf actress to win an Oscar. The award was for her performance in the film Children of a Lesser God - which also starred her real life partner at the time William Hurt. In her memoir years later, Matlin said that after the Oscars ceremony a jealous Hurt screamed abuse at her and said she didn't deserve the award. In the book she also accused him of rape and said he was a violent and angry man who hit her on occasion. Matlin said in her memoir that if you watch Children of a Lesser God you can see bruises on her legs in one scene. She said these were caused by fights with William Hurt.

In 1987, the actor Matthew Broderick took a vacation in Europe with his girlfriend (and actress) Jennifer Grey. While driving in Northern Ireland, Broderick dove straight into a car that contained Anna Gallagher, 28, and her mother Margaret Doherty, 63. Anna and Margaret were both killed in the accident. Is it believed that Broderick might have unwittingly been driving on the wrong side of the road while in the British Isles. Broderick was also injured in the crash and spent three weeks in hospital. Broderick could (and arguably should) have faced a prison sentence for dangerous driving but somehow got off with a light fine. The family of the victims were outraged by this. Martin Doherty, who is the brother of Margaret and the sister of Anna, said that he was supposed to meet Broderick in 2003 to get 'closure' but that Brodrick never turned up. In 2012 the surviving relatives of Margaret and Anna were rather appalled when Matthew Broderick featured in a car commercial for Honda.

The director Brett Ratner, who was responsible for films like the Rush Hour series with Jackie Chan, Red Dragon, and X-Men 3, is pretty disgraced in Hollywood these days. In 2018, Warner Brothers severed their deal with Ratner because of sexual misconduct allegations against him. The actresses Natasha Henstridge and Olivia Munn both said that Ratner indecently exposed himself to them. Another actress, Katharine Towne, said she was left shaken after Ratner made aggressive and unsolicited sexual advances towards her. Jaime Ray Newman, another actress, said she sat next to Ratner on a plane once and he was crude and obnoxious and showed her pornographic pictures. Eri Sasaki, who was 21 when she appeared as a bikini clad extra in Rush Hour 2, said that Ratner touched her without consent and implied that he would make her famous if she slept with him.

During production of the 1997 film Pleasantville, camera assistant Brent Lon Hershman died after falling asleep at the wheel of his car. Hershman had just completed an exhausting nineteen hour shift on the film. His widow took legal action against New Line Cinema and claimed that the crew were forced to work these punishing shifts simply so that the film could be finished more quickly to save the studio money. A number of Hollywood stars supported the legal action's suggestion that crews should not be allowed to work any shift that surpassed fourteen hours.

Leaked Sony emails revealed that director David O Russell was so demanding and rude to Amy Adams on the set of American Hustle that she fled the set in tears more than once. Her co-star Christian Bale had to intervene and warn Russell about his conduct. Russell had form when it came to this sort of thing. When he directed Three Kings, George Clooney got so annoyed at the disrespectful way that Russell treated the crew and extras that they came to blows at one point. "I would not stand for him humiliating and yelling and screaming at crew members, who weren't allowed to defend themselves," said Clooney of the Three Kings production. "I don't believe in it and it makes me crazy. So my job was then to humiliate the people who were doing the humiliating."

The leaked Sony emails on American Hustle were especially embarrassing for the studio because the leaks revealed that Amy Adams and Jennifer Lawrence were both paid less on the movie than their male co-stars. Bradley Cooper, Christian Bale, and Jeremy Renner all earned more than Adams and Lawrence on the movie's back-end compensation. Even the director David O Russell had a bigger profit sharing deal than Adams and Lawrence.

Corey Haim was a big child/teen star in the mid to late 1980s (his films included The Lost Boys and Silver Bullet) but found life in Hollywood much tougher when he got a few years older and aged out of the teen roles. Haim was addicted to drugs and ended up threatening his manager with a gun. He was then handed a past-due tax bill and sued by his insurance company for not disclosing his drug addiction. The money Haim had earned from his movies was all gone and he end up shuttling in and out of rehab. On March 10, 2010, he died at Providence Saint Joseph Medical Center of an apparent overdose. He was 38 years-old. A lot of people thought it was pretty shabby that Haim didn't feature in the 'In Memoriam' section of the Oscars when he died. It was a classic example of how you can be really famous in Hollywood for a time and then completely forgotten.

While making the classic film Chinatown, lead actress Faye Dunaway and director Roman Polanski quickly grew to loathe one another and argue all the time. Things became very tense and bitter between them in the end. Polanski eventually refused to give Dunaway any direction and simply told her to say the words in the script. They had reached the point where they couldn't even talk to each other in a civil fashion. The feud reached its apex when Dunaway peed in a plastic cup and then threw it at Polanski. Production of the film Wall Street was made a nightmare for Oliver Stone thanks to Sean Young. Young spent half the production complaining that her part wasn't big enough and lobbying to be switched to the role played by Daryl Hannah. Stone got so fed up with Sean Young that in the end he simply cut most of her scenes from the film and left her with a very minor part in the movie.

It is quite rare for an actor from the world of porn to make the 'crossover' and become a successful Hollywood actor. One person who did manage to do this was Traci Lords. Lords appeared in hundreds of porn films as a teenager but forged a new career as a 'straight' actor and won parts in high profile shows and films like Gilmore Girls, Roseanne, Married... With Children, Melrose Place, Tales from the Crypt, Will & Grace, Blade, Serial Mom, Zack and Miri Make a Porno, and Cry Baby. David Cronenberg cast porn star Marilyn Chambers in his horror film Rabid but it did not lead to a mainstream career for Chambers. Chambers, who desperately wanted to be a mainstream actress, said she met Jack Nicholson to discuss a part in Goin' South (a comedy western Nicholson was directing) but that Nicholson simply asked her if she had any cocaine and kept grilling her for information about her porn career.

Someone who has been more successful than Chambers in moving from porn to mainstream entertainment is Sasha Grey. Grey played the lead role in Steven Soderbergh's The Girlfriend Experience. One of the most bizarre and surprising career changes of any actor concerned Stephen Geoffreys. You may recall Geoffreys as William Ragsdale's eccentric spiky haired friend Edward "Evil Ed" Thompson in the cult 1985 horror film Fright Night. Geoffreys went on to appear in At Close Range with Sean Penn and also Steven Spielberg's Amazing Stories. In the 1990s though, Geoffreys began a new career as a gay porn actor and appeared in numerous porn films under the name Sam Ritter. Geoffreys has made a return to 'straight' acting but only in a very minor capacity in low-budget horror films. It is believed that Geofreys became disheartened with Hollywood because he was never cast as the lead and always had to play the eccentric supporting role.

Mia Farrow was tearfully on the brink of quitting the film Rosemary's Baby at one point to save her marriage to Frank Sinatra. With Rosemary's Baby falling behind schedule, Sinatra wanted her to quit to make a film called The Detective with him and warned the producer Robert Evans in phone calls that he better deliver her on time. To keep his star, Evans showed Farrow an hour of Rosemary's Baby and told her she was on course for an Oscar. A furious Sinatra then had divorce papers delivered on the set but Farrow had her revenge when Rosemary's Baby was a much bigger hit than Sinatra's film. Farrow even suggested to Evans they take out an ad contrasting the box-office figures.

Victor Salva is best known for directing the first three films in the Jeepers Creepers horror franchise. During the production of his 1988 film Clownhouse, Salva sexually abused 12 year-old child actor Nathan Winters. Salva even filmed one of their sexual encounters. He was convicted and sentenced to 3 years in prison. The police also found child pornography in Salva's home. However, Salva was released from prison after fifteen months in 1992 and a few years later directed a $10 million Disney movie called Powder.

When protesters (including Nathan Winters) pointed out that Salva was a paedophile and called for a boycott of his films, Disney claimed that they had no knowledge of his past when they hired him. This was taken with a huge grain of salt.

Salva is a protege of Francis Ford Coppola and it is speculated that Coppola might have pulled a few strings to get Salva some work again. Coppola would later serve as executive producer on Salva's Jeepers Creepers 2. Salva continues to direct films and while none of these have been a huge hit he has worked with some fairly famous names like Nick Nolte, Rose McGowan, and Tobin Bell. When Salva's Jeepers Creepers III was released in 2017, a despairing Nathan Winters said "To be honest with you, I feel like everything I've done to raise awareness and remind people of his crime and the abuse that I've been through has been suppressed all along. It's been a constant uphill battle."

In 2014, a film called Midnight Rider was shooting in Georgia. The film required a scene where William Hurt's character has a dream that he is in bed on some railroad tracks. Despite not securing permission, the director Randall Miller decided to shoot this scene on a real rural railway bridge. William Hurt had severe misgivings about the scene but was told it would be fine. Nothing could be further from the truth. As the scene was being shot, a real train suddenly appeared and thundered towards Hurt and the crew on the tracks. They all scrambled for safety but - tragically - camera assistant Sarah Jones was struck by the train and lost her life. Randall Miller later pleaded guilty to felony involuntary manslaughter and criminal trespass and spent a year in prison.

Woody Allen seems to be an outcast in America these days thanks to allegations that have dogged him on and off since 1992. At the start of the 1990s, Allen was in a relationship with Mia Farrow. Farrow had replaced Diane Keaton as Allen's muse and leading lady. Allen and Farrow were not married and did not live together. They both had apartments in Manhattan. Allen lived alone while Farrow lived with a large group of children she had adopted. These children included Dylan (a four year-old girl Allen and Farrow had adopted), Satchel (Mia's son and Allen's only biological child), and Soon-Yi Previn (Farrow's 21 year-old adopted daughter from her former marriage to the composer Andre Previn). Satchel Farrow would later change his name to Ronan Farrow and become a famous journalist. Woody Allen was a regular visitor to the Farrow apartment and would often go there to have breakfast with the children.

The relationship between Woody Allen and Mia Farrow was shattered in 1992 when it came to light that Allen had been having a secret relationship with her adopted daughter Soon-Yi. It is this part of the Woody Allen scandal that is still inaccurately reported. Soon-Yi was not Allen's daughter. He had not adopted Soon-Yi. Woody Allen barely knew Soon-Yi until she was a teenager. Soon-Yi was not an innocent or underage victim. She was a ferociously intelligent 21 year-old student who spoke several languages. Mia Farrow, nonetheless, was understandably furious to learn that Allen and Soon-Yi had been in a romantic relationship.

A custody battle over Satchel and Dylan began and the custody battle went nuclear when Mia Farrow accused Allen of sexually molesting Dylan. The molestation is alleged to have taken place at Mia Farrow's country home. Allen supposedly took Dylan up into the attic and fondled her private parts while she watched an electric train set go round and round. Two separate state authorities investigated the claim and neither collected sufficient evidence to take the matter any further. They noted that Dylan showed signs of 'coaching' in her taped testimony as if someone was instructing her on what to say. It was also reported that Woody Allen had passed a lie detector test.

In the aftermath of the case, Woody Allen lost contact with Satchel and Dylan (this would be a lifelong estrangement). Allen went back to making films and the scandal passed. This all changed in the wake of MeToo when (the now adult) Dylan resurfaced and repeated the claim that Woody Allen had molested her when she was a child. Dylan enjoyed the considerable support of Ronan Farrow. Ronan had been important in exposing Harvey Weinstein and now had his estranged father in his sights. Just to add another bizarre note to this story, the adult Ronan looked uncannily like Frank Sinatra did as a young man. Sinatra was Mia Farrow's former husband and it seems incredibly likely that Sinatra and not Woody Allen is Ronan's biological father. In an article for the New York Times, Allen, only half in jest, wondered aloud why he had paid all that child support to Ronan if the kid's father was Frank Sinatra.

In the wake of Dylan and Ronan's reactivation of the 1992 claims, a raft of actors distanced themselves from Woody Allen and said they would never work with him again. Amazon terminated their contract with Allen and he was forced to make his new film in Spain. Woody Allen is now lumped in with the likes of Bill Cosby and Harvey Weinstein and yet (unlike Cosby and Weinstein) has never been convicted of anything. Cosby and Weinstein had dozens of people come forward to accuse them of abuse but the one solitary accusation aimed at Woody Allen derived from an embittered partner who he was in a custody battle with.

Moses Farrow, another of Mia's children, was in the house when Woody Allen was alleged to have molested Dylan. Moses thinks the allegation is ludicrous and points out that the attic never even had a train set up there (the train set is always mentioned by Dylan when she recalls her molestation). According to Moses Farrow, the attic was so small you couldn't even get up there let alone set up a train set and still have room to molest someone. Moses has called Mia Farrow an abusive mother and thinks that Dylan was coached into the abuse allegation as Mia's revenge on Allen.

Dylan, for her part, genuinely seems to believe she was abused. But is she telling the truth or the victim of a false memory implanted by her mother? The Farrow family was deathly silent when Mia's brother was convicted of child abuse and there was also the curious public support that Mia Farrow has always offered Roman Polanski. Unlike Woody Allen, Polanski is a proven child sex abuser. If the molestation of Dylan really happened, why on earth would Mia be supporting Roman Polanski? And yet, despite the lack of clarity and surplus of doubt in this case, Woody Allen remains guilty in the great court of tittle tattle and gossip. The internet is still full of speculative and inaccurate articles which depict him as a prolific child abuser who married his own daughter.

Arnold Schwarzenegger has a love child named Joseph Baena as a result of an affair with his former housekeeper Mildred Baena. Joseph looks remarkably like his famous father. Arnold had to tell his wife about the affair during the time that he left acting for politics. In 2013, The Big Bang Theory star Kaley Cuoco was photographed holding hands with Henry Cavill. The media smelt a rat because both of these actors had the same PR firm. Sure enough, it was all a publicity stunt to boost the profile of the duo. The perplexing thing about the PR stunt is that one wouldn't have thought these two needed a boost. Cavill was the new Superman and Cuoco was in one of the most popular TV shows in America.

The Irish actor Stuart Townsend was once a rapidly rising star set to become a big name in Hollywood. His biggest break came when he was cast as Aragorn in Lord of the Rings for Peter Jackson. The three Lord of the Rings films were huge hits and would have made Townsend a big star. However, he never got to appear in them. As the production of the first film was about to begin, Peter Jackson suddenly decided that Townsend was too young to play Aragorn and replaced him with Viggo Mortensen. Townsend was absolutely furious. Anthony Daniels and Kenny Baker, who played C-3PO and R2D2 in the Star Wars films, hated each other in real life. The late Kenny Baker said that Daniels was always rude and condescending to him. The actress Amy Hill said that Mike Myers was the worst person she had ever worked with. Hill had the misfortune to appear in the megabomb The Cat in the Hat. Hill said that Myers was weird and reclusive and had flunkies who would race onto the set to feed him chocolate.

James Remar was originally cast as Corporal Hicks in the classic science fiction sequel Aliens. Remar began shooting the movie at Pinewood Studios in London but his drug problems soon made his participation in Aliens untenable. When word got around that Remar was trawling through London pubs trying to score cocaine, he was removed from the production and sent home. Michael Biehn was flown over to replace him. Biehn thought that Aliens, which gave him a rare chance to play a heroic character, might make him a star but he was to be disappointed in this ambition. Biehn was furious when he learned that he wasn't going to be in Alien 3. When he learned that a dummy of him was being used in Alien 3 to depict the early death of Hicks in a shuttle crash, Biehn got his management to secure a fee for the use of his likeness.

Film producer Julia Phillips famously burned her bridges on Hollywood with the bitchy memoir You'll Never Eat Lunch in this Town Again. The 650-page "hate letter to Hollywood" spared no one in Tinseltown. Spielberg was a "selfish, egomaniacal and greedy nerd"; Goldie Hawn "borderline dirty with stringy hair"; Warren Beatty, she alleged, had suggested a threesome with Phillips and her 14-year-old daughter; the producer Larry Gordon was a "loudmouth"; Joel Silver a "fat slob". The writer Erica Jong resembled "Miss Piggy when her face is in repose"; and the agent Michael (The "Valley Viper") Ovitz had no interest in the outside world unless it involved "a two-picture deal for one of his clients".

Although she was at the time attempting to revive her career by developing Anne Rice's novel Interview with the Vampire for the studio boss David Geffen, Julia Phillips ventured the opinion that he had a "collagened face" that made him look like "a middle-aged baby".

Paparazzi are often the bane of celebrity lives but Hollywood celebrities also use paparazzi to their advantage. Some actors and celebrities have their own photographers who they pay to come and photograph them at events. This not only makes them appear more in demand and famous but also gives them control over the pictures. Ben Affleck is one of many actors who has been accused of having personal paparazzi who he hires to photograph him in staged 'happy' family events.

In an interview, Tatum O'Neal, said that Bruce Willis was the worst person she had ever worked with. "Off the top of my head, I'd say Bruce Willis. He was so rude to me I was shocked. Usually people are respectful to me just because I've been around so long, but he wasn't. He seemed to be very taken with himself and his own celebrity. He was such an ass I couldn't believe it. He thinks he's special. He's not a cool guy."

Drew Barrymore was in many ways the original Hollywood wild child. Born into a famous acting dynasty, she became one of the most well known child actors of her era thanks to films like E.T and Firestarter. By the age of nine though she began to drink alcohol and by the age of thirteen had started taking cocaine. Barrymore's career seemed pretty much over at one point. Her parents tried to have her put in an institution and she ended up in rehab. In 1994, Barrymore married a Los Angeles bar owner called Jeremy Thomas and the marriage lasted all of two months. Barrymore peered over the edge of oblivion but miraculously managed to survive her troubled youth and emerge as a powerful and stable producer and actor in Hollywood.

In 2015, Jim Carrey's former girlfriend, Cathriona White, was found dead of a prescription drug overdose. The tragic death was ruled a suicide. Carrey was a pallbearer at the funeral and seemed devastated. Two people who were not impressed by Carey's show of grief was White's husband and mother. They filed a lawsuit against Jim Carrey in which they alleged he had supplied the drugs which killed Cathriona. The lawsuit also claimed that Carrey had given Cathriona White a number of sexually transmitted diseases during their time together.

Chuck Wepner was a heavyweight boxer in the sixties and seventies. Wepner was what you might call a fringe contender or a journeyman. He was tough but a notch below the best in the division. In 1975, Wepner was an unlikely challenger to world heavyweight champion Muhammad Ali and lasted to the 15th round. Wepner even had a small moment of glory when he stepped on Ali's foot and the resulting tumble was mistakenly scored as a knockdown for Wepner. One person who watched the Ali-Wepner fight was a struggling young actor named Sylvester Stallone. The sight of this overmatched plucky white clubfighter fighting Muhammad Ali inspired

Stallone to write Rocky. Stallone also promised Wepner that he would give him a break in Hollywood and cast him in one of his films.

Wepner later auditioned for a role in Rocky II but was not given the part. Wepner had further cause for complaint when Rocky III featured Stallone fighting Hulk Hogan (as Thunderlips) in a boxer v wrestler contest. In 1976, Wepner had participated in a boxer v wrestler clash against André the Giant and even been thrown out of the ring (which Thunderlips also does to Rocky Balboa in Rocky III). Wepner could be forgiven for believing that Stallone was using his life for material in the Rocky films.

Years later, Wepner learned that Stallone was shooting Copland in New Jersey near where he lived and was infuriated that Stallone had not got in touch or found a small part in the film for him. Over the decades since Rocky came out, Wepner has attempted various legal actions which seek to claim that Rocky was based on his own life and that he was never given any credit for this. Stallone has never though confirmed that Rocky was at least partly based on Chuck Wepner - although clearly it was.

The actress Kathryn Rossetter said that Dustin Hoffman groped her frequently when they appeared in Death of a Salesman on Broadway in 1983. The writer Anna Graham Hunter, who was a teenage intern at the time, said that during production of the TV movie version of the play, Hoffman repeatedly groped her backside and engaged in lewd sex chat in front of her. In response to these claims, offman said - "I have the utmost respect for women and feel terrible that anything I might have done could have put her in an uncomfortable situation. I am sorry. It is not reflective of who I am." Several women have now accused Hoffman of sexually inappropriate behaviour in the past. Hoffman has denied the allegations.

Paramount claimed that the hit 1988 Eddie Murphy comedy

Coming to America hadn't made any profit despite it clocking up nearly $300 million in box-office receipts. As a result of this 'creative accounting', they refused to pay the writer Art Buchwald the profit share deal he had arranged in his contract. A furious Buchwald successfully sued Paramount and won $900,000. The tactic of Paramount in trying to avoid paying Art Buchwald any profits is known in the film and television industry as 'Hollywood Accounting'. There are many examples of Hollywood Accounting. Sigourney Weaver was told that she wouldn't get her royalties on Ghostbusters because the film hadn't gone into profit. This was a remarkable claim considering the film was one of the biggest hits of 1984! Weaver threatened legal action and was placated by the promise of a bigger financial deal for Ghostbusters II.

The late Stan Lee also experienced Hollywood Accounting. He had a contract that entitled him to a share of the profits from 2002's Spider-Man but Sony (ludicrously) tried to get out of paying him by claiming the film didn't make a profit. The reason why Cary Elwes didn't return for the initial Saw sequels that he felt he had been stiffed by Lionsgate Films. Despite being on a profit share deal for Saw and the film becoming a huge hit, Elwes never actually saw any of the money. Elwes later patched things up with the studio and made an appearance again later in the franchise.

David Prowse, who was inside the Darth Vadar suit in the original Star Wars films, said in 2009 that he had yet to receive any royalties for the 1983 entry Return of the Jedi. "I get these occasional letters from Lucasfilm saying that we regret to inform you that as Return of the Jedi has never gone into profit, we've got nothing to send you. Now here we're talking about one of the biggest releases of all time, I don't want to look like I'm bitching about it, but on the other hand, if there's a pot of gold somewhere that I ought to be having a share of, I would like to see it."

Michael Moore took Miramax Films to court when they tried to stiff him on the profit share deal he had for his documentary

Fahrenheit 9/11. The matter was settled out of court. Moore is a documentary filmmaker who rails against capitalism, inequality, greed, and the wealthy in his films. Guess what? Moore's divorce case later revealed that he had $50 million in the bank and owned nine houses. He still makes documentaries but no one watches them anymore.

Another victim of Hollywood Accounting was Winston Groom. Groom wrote the novel Forrest Gump - which became a blockbuster film in 1994. The film made nearly $700 million but Groom ended up with a paltry £300,000. This left such a bad taste that Groom never did a deal to allow Hollywood to film his Forest Gump sequel novel. Tom Hanks, by contrast, earned about $65 million from his profit share deal on Forrest Gump. The absurdity of Hollywood Accounting is best illustrated an accounting report that Warners Bros issued after the release of Harry Potter and The Order of the Phoenix. Despite the fact that the film had grossed nearly one billion dollars at the time of the report, Warner Bros insisted that the movie was still in the red and hadn't made any money yet!

The creator and writer J. Michael Straczynski said he was a victim of Hollywood Accounting on his cult sci-fi show Babylon 5 and never saw any of the profits the show made. "The show, all in, cost about $110 million to make. Each year of its original run, we know it showed a profit because they TOLD us so. And in one case, they actually showed us the figures. It's now been on the air worldwide for ten years. There's been merchandise, syndication, cable, books, you name it. The DVDs grossed roughly half a BILLION dollars (and that was just after they put out S5, without all of the S5 sales in). So what does my last profit statement say? We're $80 million in the red. Basically, by the terms of my contract, if a set on a WB movie burns down in Botswana, they can charge it against B5's profits." Rysher Entertainment, who made the TV show Nash Bridges, tried to avoid paying any royalties to the lead actor Don Johnson by claiming that the show never made a profit. This was the old familiar ploy of Hollywood Accounting in action again. Johnson sued Rysher

Entertainment and won $23 million.

Tobe Hooper was the director of the classic 1982 horror film Poltergeist. This film was written and produced by Steven Spielberg and stories persist that he secretly directed most of it. Spielberg was prepping E.T at the time and his studio contract forbode him from directing another film. This is why he asked Texas Chainsaw Massacre director Tobe Hooper to direct his Poltergeist script. Spielberg was on the set of Poltergeist a lot and later seemed to suggest he had made all the major decisions because Tobe Hopper wasn't a 'take charge' sort of person.

Spielberg later had to apologise to Hooper in The Hollywood Reporter for suggesting that he (Spielberg) had made the film himself. The stories that Spielberg secretly directed Poltergeist stem a lot by comments by Zelda Rubenstein - one of the stars of the film. Rubenstein said that Spielberg had directed all the scenes she took part in. Rubenstein also said that Hooper was out of his head on drugs during her time on the set. Other actors in the cast have disputed Rubenstein's account and defended Tobe Hooper. Whatever the actual truth, Poltergeist feels an awful lot like a Steven Spielberg film at times. If any film feels like Dark Amblin it is surely Poltergeist.

River Phoenix met his end in 1993 outside of the Viper Room - a Los Angeles nightclub owned by Johnny Depp. Phoenix was one of the mot famous young stars in Hollywood and destined for a long and lucrative career. He was often compared to James Dean and famous for films like Stand By Me and Indiana Jones and the Last Crusade. Phoenix was only 23 when he died of a drugs overdose outside of the Viper Room. Phoenix was always regarded to be one of the most clean cut stars in Hollywood. He was a vegan environmentalist who was said to avoid alcohol and his family were famous for avoiding the Hollywood limelight. And yet, in reality, Phoenix was the tragic cliche of a young Hollywood star. He and his friends were frequent users of hard drugs and loved trawling seedy nightclubs. Phoenix died after injecting a 'speedball' of heroin and cocaine. His last words were - "I don't feel so good. I think I'm OD'ing."

When it comes to the sexuality of actors in Hollywood, things have happily changed for the better. If Rock Hudson was around today he would not have to pretend he wasn't gay. Actors like Luke Evans are openly gay today and it isn't a big deal at all. There are though still actors in the closet - which has led to much speculation and rumour. John Travolta has often been reported to be gay but he has never confessed to this. The late Carrie Fisher said that everyone knew Travolta was gay and Travolta's former pilot said he had a six year relationship with the star. Travolta was also accused of groping a 21 year-old male masseur according to a leaked police report. Tom Cruise has also dodged rumours about his sexuality and once sued a French magazine which ran a story about him having an affair with a man.

The late Kelly Preston was engaged to Charlie Sheen before she married John Travolta. Their engagement was understandably called off when Sheen somehow managed to shoot Preston in the arm. Sheen said that Preston picked up some of his clothes and his gun fell out and then went off. Preston however never gave her side of the story. She had to go to hospital for shrapnel wounds. If you want to hold onto a boyfriend or husband it's probably best to keep them away from Angelina Jolie. Billy Bob Thornton left his girlfriend Laura Dern to marry Jolie after they made the film Pushing Tin. Jolie struck again years later when she stole Brad Pitt from his wife Jennifer Anniston after they met making the film Mr & Mrs Smith. The actress Isla Fisher could easily have been killed on the 2013 film Now You See Me where her escapologist character had to escape from a tank of water. Fisher got stuck in the tank and couldn't signal for help. She had to hold her breath for two minutes before help arrived.

The makers of the 1987 film Hellraiser were very annoyed when the famous British film critic Barry Norman (who had a weekly film review show on the BBC) trashed the movie. They were especially irritated because it was for all and intents and purposes a British film industry movie and they felt as if Norman should be more supportive. As a consequence of this they invited Norman to visit the set of Hellraiser II. During his visit Barry Norman confessed to them that he just didn't like horror movies - which would explain why he'd hated Hellraiser. Norman conceded to them though that films should be judged on their individual merit - regardless of what genre they fell into.

Paul Bateson was a former radiographer who appeared in the famous horror movie The Exorcist (during the hospital scene). Bateson was later a suspect in the case of a serial killer who was never captured. The 'bag murders' was the name given to a spate of killings in New York from 1975 to 1977. There were six murders in all. The victims were cut up before their remains were shoved in a bag and thrown in the Hudson River. As a consequence of this it was impossible to identify the victims and capturing the killer (who is generally known as The Greenwich Village Killer) proved equally complicated. The only lead the police had to go on was to place the clothing found on the remains under scrutiny.

They managed to deduce that the victims seemed to be wearing items purchased from leather stores in Greenwich Village - specifically a fetish shop on Christopher Street. The location was a common haunt for the local gay community and so it seemed logical to presume that the victims were gay men. While this all certainly narrowed down the lines of the investigation the inability to identify the victims was obviously a tremendous hindrance to the police. There was a suspect (of sorts) though in the end when it came to these harrowing murders. The suspect was Paul Bateson. Bateson seemed to fall on hard times after The Exorcist and began drinking a lot. Things got so bad he ended up working in a porno cinema. Bateson was arrested in 1977 for the murder of a reporter named Addison Verrill. Verill covered the film scene for Variety and had been beaten and stabbed in his apartment. The police suspected at the time that it was a robbery and financially motivated.

Bateson lived in Greenwich Village and frequented leather bars in the district. He was found guilty of Verrill's murder but during the trial the prosecution alleged that Bateson had confessed to other murders and said that he dismembered his victims and put them in bags. When one added all these details together then Bateson was a pretty strong suspect in the 'bag murders' investigation. The judge at the trial though dismissed the prosecution's attempt to portray Bateson as a serial killer and said the connections between the murder in question and other murders were too vague to be admissible. Bateson was found guilty of the murder of Addison Verrill but (despite reports to the contrary) he has never confessed to being the person responsible for the bag murders and insists that he is innocent.

Bateson apparently got out of prison in 2005. The police simply never had sufficient evidence to build a case against him for the bag murders. Sadly, because it was so long ago and the victims were impossible to identify the true identity of the killer may never be known. It could be that Bateson was The Greenwich Village Killer or it could have been someone else. The case of Paul Bateson loosely inspired the William Friedkin film Cruising. He was also depicted in the David Fincher television show Manhunter.

In the 1980s, Jennifer Grey was a successful movie actress well known for films like Ferris Bueller's Day Off, Dirty Dancing and Red Dawn. However, in the early 1990s she did something unfathomable which killed her career stone dead. Grey underwent two rhinoplasty procedures. In simple terms, she had a nose job. After the operations, Grey looked completely different. So now, prospective employers were not getting the Jennifer Grey of Dirty Dancing fame. They were getting a woman who looked nothing like Jennifer Grey! Not surprisingly, Grey's career suffered. She went from being a movie star to starring in obscure TV movies and making an appearance on Dancing with the Stars. "I went in the operating theatre a celebrity - and come out anonymous. It was like being in a witness protection program or being invisible. I remember going to a restaurant where I had been going for years. I ran into people I knew and would say, 'Hey.' Nothing. I'll always be this once-famous actress nobody recognises... because of a nose job."

Ashleigh Aston Moore appeared in the 1995 film Now and Then when she was fourteen - for which she won a YTV Achievement Award. She had been acting since she was eleven and had also appeared in TV shows like Northern Exposure. Her last credit was an episode of Touched By An Angel in 1997. After that she drifted out of acting and vanished into obscurity. In 2007 she died of a heroin overdose at the age of 26. It seems that Moore, like a number of child stars who have fallen on hard times, tried to use drugs to fill the hole left by the loss of fame and an acting career. Brad Renfro was discovered at age 10 by director Joel Schumacher and cast in The Client with Susan Sarandon and Tommy Lee Jones. He went on to star in films like Apt Pupil and Sleepers. In 1998 Renfro was arrested for cocaine possession and in 2000 he attempted to steal a yacht from Fort Lauderdale harbor. Renfro had other charges for underage drinking and heroin possession. He died of a heroin overdose in 2008 at the age of 25. It was a tragic and all too familiar waste of a Hollywood career that had begun so promisingly.

Jake Lloyd played young Anakin Skywalker in the 1999 film Star Wars: Episode I – The Phantom Menace. Lloyd was only eight when cast. You might think this was a dream part but nothing could be farther from the truth. Lloyd and the film were both panned in reviews and he grew to hate Star Wars. He made two more films and then retired from acting. He was monosyllabic and sarcastic in interviews and clearly an unhappy and troubled young man. In 2015, Lloyd was arrested for reckless driving, driving without a license, and resisting arrest. There were stories that he attacked his mother and that he was in an institution.

Mischa Barton first came to prominence at the age of eleven with an impressive performance in the cult film Lawn Dogs. She then had parts in Knotting Hill and The Sixth Sense and studied acting at The Royal Academy of Dramatic Art in London. A great career seemed to be ahead of Barton but she made a surprising move when she signed to be in the teen drama The OC in 2003. After she left the show, Barton's acting career literally went nowhere fast. She was arrested for drink driving, was filmed having blazing arguments with her mother, ended up in hospital for drinking while on antibiotics, and was arrested for driving without a licence. Just to finish it all off, a sex tape featuring Barton surfaced in 2017 and she had to fight to stop its release. These days, Barton can be seen in bargain basement horror movies and reality shows. She is sad proof that a precocious child actor doesn't always become a successful actor when they grow-up.

Brandon Lee was the handsome son of the legendary Bruce Lee and began a promising career in Hollywood with action roles. Brandon's movies (Legacy of Rage, Laser Mission, Showdown in Little Tokyo, Rapid Fire) hadn't got great reviews but the critics were quite kind to him and said he was charismatic and likeable onscreen and had a good future in Hollywood. 1992's Rapid Fire was sort of like the first undiluted Brandon Lee film and suggested he could follow in the footsteps of people like Steven Seagal and Chuck Norris. Lee had an advantage over them too in that he looked a bit like Johnny Depp and was much younger.

Brandon signed on next to appear in a film called The Crow - which was something of a departure. The Crow was a superhero film with horror elements and was considerably more ambitious than any film Brandon had been in before. Sadly, this would turn out to be Brandon's last film. He was killed shooting The Crow when a live primer in a dummy round hit him at point blank range during a gun sequence. He was only 28 years-old. The tragic accident happened on March 31, 1993. There were only eight days left on filming on the movie and Brandon was due to get married in the following few weeks when production on The Crow had concluded. The actor Michael Masse, who played a villain in The Crow, was part of a scene in which his character shot Brandon's character. When the stunt was concluded the crew became aware that Brandon was not moving. There was now a hole in his abdomen and he was rushed to hospital. Despite six hours of surgery he died of his injuries.

The accident had occurred because the bullets used in the gun had been converted to blanks from live bullets. Blanks are supposed to have cardboard tips so that in the event of any accidental contact the damage is minimal. In this case though one of the lead tips from the modified live bullets was still in the gun and came loose during the scene - fatally hitting Brandon in the stomach. It was basically incompetence on the part of the people making the film. The death was ruled an accident but Brandon's mother Linda Lee Cadwell launched a civil suit against the film studio - which was eventually settled out of court.

The Crow turned out to be a pretty good film but this was obviously scant consolation to the late Brandon Lee and his distraught family. The Crow might well have made Brandon Lee a big star had he lived but - alas - we'll never know how his career would panned out now. The Crow was completed with the use of a double after Brandon's death. This was a rather spooky echo of how Bruce Lee's last film (Game of Death) was completed with a double after Bruce Lee died. It is sometimes said that Brandon fell victim to a family curse but this is patently fiction. The Crow was apparently quite an incompetent production and - sadly - it was safety issues on the set which cost Brandon Lee his life.

TALES FROM OLD HOLLYWOOD

The much loved Swedish actress Ingrid Bergman created a scandal in 1950 when she left her husband for the film director Roberto Rossellini. Believe it or not, Bergman was even called an 'apostle of degradation' by American politicians and banned from appearing on the Ed Sullivan Show. Although it all sounds absolutely preposterous today, the scandal derived from the fact that Bergman was known for playing saintly 'good girl' roles and so it apparently came as a shock to the American public that she was just a normal person in real life and nothing like her screen characters. Bergman moved to Italy as a consequence and was effectively banished from the United States for ten years. Bergman later said that she thought the scandal was all rather silly and that she didn't regret anything she had done during this time.

Errol Flynn's Malibu beach house was dubbed 'cirrhosis by the sea' by Carole Lombard because of the copious amount of partying and drinking that went on. Flynn was also, according to his debauched legend, something of a peeping Tom. In her memoir, Hedy Lamarr said that Flynn's house was full of peepholes and opaque glass so that one could spy on whoever was in the bathroom or bedrooms. The tabloid scandal mag Confidential reported in an article that Flynn had a large mirror on the ceiling of one of the bedrooms where it was possible to spy on the bed below from the attic. Flynn took legal action against Confidential but later admitted in his autobiography that the ceiling mirror story was in fact true. However, Flynn claimed that the mirror was never actually used to impose on anyone's privacy. It's safe to say that no one really believed Flynn had never used the mirror to spy on his unwitting guests.

Shirley Temple began her career in Baby Burlesks. These were pre-code films made in the years before Hollywood had established a moral censorship code for productions to abide by. Baby Burlesks were essentially film pastiches in which the cast are all children but dressed up as adults (sort of like Bugsy Malone). These short films are troubling today and quite bizarre. In one of the shorts Shirley Temple plainly appears to be playing a prostitute and the African-American kids were sometimes dressed up as natives from the jungle. Temple said that if any of the kids misbehaved on these films they had to and sit on a block of ice as punishment.

When she was seventeen, Shirley Temple was warned by Anita Colby, the executive of David O Selznick, that if she ever encountered Selznick in leggings she should be very wary because he usually donned this attire when he wanted to make a sexual advance to an actress. Sure enough, Temple had real life experience of this predatory custom. 'Coming around my side of the desk, he reached and took my hand in his,' wrote Temple in her memoir. 'Glancing down, I saw the telltale stocking feet. Pulling free, I turned for the door, but even more quickly he reached back over the edge of his desk and flicked a switch I had learned from Colby was a remote door-locking device. I was trapped. Like the cartoon of wolf and piglet, once again we circled and reversed directions around his furniture. Blessed with the agility of a young dancer and confronted by an amorous but overweight producer, I had little difficulty avoiding passionate clumsiness.'

Shirley Temple said that when she was a teen actress, the comedian George Jessel made an unsolicited sexual advance. 'We were standing a pace separated, eyeball to eyeball. In one quick development he opened his pants and, with an unexpected reach, circled me with one arm... I could feel his other hand grabbing to lift my shirt. Little could I do but thrust my right knee upward into his groin... Pain, disgust, and hate flickered across his face, but I felt no mercy. More and more the adult movie business seemed populated with a bunch of copulating tomcats.'

Wizard of Oz star Judy Garland had a pretty awful time in Hollywood by all accounts. When she was still a teenager, the studio decided she was too fat and so took extraordinary measures to control her weight. She was put on a diet of coffee and soup and smoked eighty cigarettes a day to curb hunger pangs. Garland was given all manner of medication - including 'uppers' and 'downers' so that she could alternately stay up for hours or go to sleep in an instant. Garland became hooked on the prescription drugs and it affected her for the rest of her life. Mickey Rooney also said that when he worked with Judy Garland they were often given pills by the studios that enabled them to work long hours without getting tired. In her memoir, Garland also recalled that, when was a teen star, studio boss Louis B. Mayer would sit her on his knee and fondle her breast.

The dwarfs who played the munchkins in The Wizard of Oz were very badly behaved and made production on the film rather difficult at times. The dwarfs liked to have a good time and would get drunk a lot. One of the crew said they had be collected up at the end of shooting because they had a habit of passing out drunk. The worst habit of the dwarfs was sticking their hand up Judy Garland's dress. Garland had to endure a lot of groping from the dwarfs over the course of the production. It is said that the dwarfs would have orgies back at their hotel after they had finished shooting scenes.

Joan Crawford, according to gossip and her own suggestive comments, was famous for sleeping around as a young sex symbol. There is a rumour about Crawford, often reported as fact, that she made some 'stag' porn films to pay the bills before she became famous and that these films were then tracked down and destroyed to protect her later on. Legend has it that some copies still exist in private collections. The titles of said films were The Casting Couch, Velvet Lips, and The Plumber. The popular myth is that Hollywood fixer Eddie Mannix spent exhaustive years tracking down all prints of the films, and paid $100,000 out of studio coffers for the original negative. Despite the many accounts of this alleged affair, it's highly possible that the Crawford sex film story was merely a phantom one. Perhaps they never existed - at least not in the explicit form that is often reported. It's likely they were tamer affairs that Crawford barely featured in. The Crawford sex film story feels like a Hollywood urban myth that caught hold and never quite got debunked. Vague whispers that the FBI knew of the films only adds to the legend, true or otherwise.

Noah's Ark is a 1928 film directed by Michael Curtiz and written by Darryl F Zanuck. This is a prime example of how appearing in a big epic film in Old Hollywood could be a dangerous line of work at the best of times. Shooting the climax of this movie involved 600,000 gallons of water and tragedy soon abounded. Five extras drowned shooting the flood sequence and there were a number of serious injuries from extras being thrown around by the water. One extra had to have a limb amputated and there were broken bones all over the place. Other thirty ambulances were required on the set and the lead actress was left with a bout of pneumonia. Noah's Ark forced Hollywood to introduce new safety standards for film productions and spare a thought for the poor extras who were risking life and limb to bring these Hollywood epics to life.

We think of plastic surgery as a modern fad but this is not the case at all. It was fairly common for aspiring stars in Old Hollywood to go under the knife and in many cases it was the studio who instigated the plastic surgery. Rita Hayworth had hairline surgery because her hairline was deemed too low. The result was a success and gave her a more classic profile and look. Marilyn Monroe had surgery on her nose and chin and dyed her brown hair blonde. The end result was a spectacular makeover. Monroe, like Hayworth, also had electrolysis to alter the shape of her hairline.

It was common for men in Old Hollywood to have work done too. Dean Martin had a nosejob and even John Wayne had a facelift. Wayne also had surgery on his neck and eyelids in an attempt to make himself look younger. Gary Cooper had a facelift and surgery on his neck to get rid of a double chin. Frank Sinatra is another actor who had numerous plastic surgeries in an attempt to hold onto his boyish looks.

Joan Crawford had her back teeth removed to give her cheekbones a more prominent look. She was told by an agent that if she didn't do this she would never get any work beyond the age of 25. In her later years, Crawford became a recluse after she saw a photograph of herself in the newspaper and was shocked at how old she looked. She decided she wanted people to remember her how she used to be so stopped going out and allowing people to photograph her. Marlene Dietrich is another actress who is believed to have teeth removed in order to alter the shape of her cheekbones.

Burt Lancaster was notorious for have many surgeries. He is believed to have had cosmetic surgery on his chin, nose, and teeth. Surgery was a lot more risky in those days but stars were desperate to improve their looks and hold onto their career so they were willing to put these risks at the back of their mind each time they visited Hollywood surgeons. Mary Pickford had plastic surgery at a young age and this is said to have a detrimental impact on her career because an actor obviously needs to have full expression in their face to perform their craft!

Clark Gable was another Old Hollywood star who had to have work done. He had his ears pinned back and extensive surgery on his teeth. Gable lost his teeth as a young man due to gum disease and wore dentures. He was said to suffer from halitosis. Kissing scenes were apparently something of an ordeal for his female co-stars. Rudolph Valentino was another star who had his ears pinned back to make them less prominent. Hedy Lamarr had a considerable amount of plastic surgery in the end - to the point where she barely looked like herself anymore. She had a facelift, nose, job, and even an early form of Botox.

Lavender marriages were a facet of Old Hollywood that seem

preposterous today. A lavender marriage was where it would be arranged by the studio for a gay actor to marry a member of the opposite sex to quash rumours about their sexuality. The most famous example of this is Rock Hudson, who was gay in real life, marrying his secretary Phyllis Gates. It is often speculated that Danny Kaye's marriage to Sylvia Fine was a lavender marriage and it has been said that Barbara Stanwyck and Robert Taylor married each other to BOTH quash rumours about their sexuality. Not everyone was willing to go along with Hollywood's attempt to mask the private lives of the stars. William Haines, who is often referred to as Hollywood's first openly gay actor, ignored pressure from studios to enter in a lavender marriage in the 1930s and saw his career come to an abrupt halt as a consequence. Haines opened up an interior design business and got out of acting altogether because he refused to lie about who he really was.

Believe it or not, it was fairly common for studios in Old Hollywood to arrange for abortions if any of their contracted actresses got pregnant - especially if the pregnancy happened out of wedlock or through an affair. Bette Davis, Joan Crawford, Judy Garland, Tallulah Bankhead, Jeanette McDonald, Lana Turner, and Dorothy Dandridge all had abortions arranged by the studios. The reason for the abortions was that the studios at the time inserted a 'morality clause' into the contracts of their stars. If an actress was involved in a scandalous (by the standards of the era) pregnancy, then this meant they had violated that morality clause. Some of these abortions had the consent of the actress (some did not want a baby to stifle their career) and some were insisted upon.

Bobby Driscoll was the voice and model of Disney's Peter Pan and won a Juvenile Academy Award in 1949. At one point he was making $50,000 a year (with inflation that equates to half a million dollars today). Driscoll however, in a familiar child star trope, blew the money on drugs and couldn't get any work when he grew up. He died in 1968 and was buried in an unmarked grave because no one knew who he was or came forward to claim the body. It was only a fingerprint match from the police station that later enabled the authorities to deduce who he really was.

Cary Grant is often alleged to have had a relationship with the actor Randolph Scott. Grant and Scott shared a house for ten years and would cook together, eat together, swim together, and give the impression of being a married couple. Grant and Scott were both in the film My Favourite Wife. Bert Granet, who worked on the script for that film, said that Grant and Scott didn't make any attempt to hide their close relationship. "We shot the pool sequence at the Huntington Hotel in Pasadena. Cary and Randy Scott arrived as a pair and, to the total astonishment of myself, the director, and the ultra-macho crew, instead of taking separate suites moved into the same room together. Everyone looked at everyone else. It seemed hardly believable."

The 1942 comedy fantasy film I Married A Witch became a troubled production thanks to the mutual dislike of its stars Fredric March and Veronica Lake. March called Lake a brainless sexpot and this was reciprocated when Lake dubbed him a pompous poseur. Because of the many scenes where March has to carry Lake in the film, the actress put weights in her dress to make this a more difficult task. Lake is said to taken the chance to knee March in the groin during more physical scenes. It's safe to say that whatever chemistry these two stars had on the screen was not carried over into reality.

Veronica Lake was one of the most iconic stars in Hollywood history but her later life was difficult and even tragic. She battled schizophrenia and alcoholism and barely acted again after 1952. In the 1960s, Lake worked as a waitress in a hotel and booze took a heavy toll on her famous looks. She made a return to acting in the trashy bargain basement horror film Flesh Feast in 1970. Lake appears drunk in the film and doesn't seem to have any teeth. This was a rather sad epilogue to one of the most famous careers in Hollywood. Lake died of acute renal failure in 1973. The doctors and nurses at the hospital were amazed that Veronica Lake never seemed to have any visitors. It felt like this legendary star had been completely forgotten. Lake's ashes remained in a funeral home for three years because no one wanted to pay any expenses.

A common question people have about Frank Sinatra concern his links to the Mafia. Was Sinatra connected to the Mob? Well, yes and no seems to be the answer but mostly yes. Sinatra was not a mobster but he was friendly with Mafia bosses and associates, this stretching back to his early days in New Jersey. Lucky Luciano arranged for him to perform at many of his parties in Havana, Sinatra even allegedly being at the 1947 Havana Conference. Luciano also borrowed two million dollars from Sinatra at one point. Sinatra did many concerts on behest of the Mob.

In 1976 Sinatra was photographed posing with Mob bosses and personalities like Paul Castellano, Joe Gambino, and 'Jimmy the Weasel' Fratianno at the Westchester Premier Theater, NYC. Sinatra's daughter Tina said that her father used Mob ties to help boost a young John F Kennedy in politics. It is often alleged that Sinatra used the Mafia to get a part in From Here to Eternity. There is some debate over this latter claim. What is certainly true is that Sinatra knew powerful Mafia figures and seemed to like associating with them at social functions or events. It seems that he found them glamorous. He did concerts for them and it seems likely the Mafia and Sinatra did each other a few favours. He flirted with Mob figures and knew them socially. You have to remember that in decades past the Mob had many tentacles in areas like showbusiness and sports. It was much harder to avoid them.

It is often alleged that Walt Disney was a fan of Cryonics and upon his death his body was frozen and placed beneath the Pirates of the Caribbean ride at Disneyland. The idea is that in the far future medical technology will be so advanced that those who died but were preserved and frozen can be thawed out and returned to full health. While the science community is somewhat dubious about Cryonics there are companies making money out of this. It transpires though that the Disney story is nothing but an urban myth that seems to have snowballed over the years. Walt Disney was actually cremated. "Walt Disney wanted to be frozen," said Bob Nelson, president of the California Cryogenics Society when Disney died in 1966. "Lots of people think that he was, and that the body's in cold storage in his basement. The truth is, Walt missed out. He never specified it in writing, and when he died the family didn't go for it. They had him cremated. I personally have seen his ashes. They're in Forest Lawn. Two weeks later we froze the first man. If Disney had been the first it would have made headlines around the world and been a real shot in the arm for cryonics. But that's the way it goes."

Wallace Reid was one of the biggest stars of the silent era. He made over a hundred short films and seemed set for a long career. He was handsome and athletic and even raced cars in his spare time. Reid was like the big action star of the era and hugely popular. In 1919, while shooting The Valley of the Giant, Reid was injured in a train crash. In order to keep the actor free of pain and able to work, he was prescribed morphine. Reid became hopelessly addicted to morphine and used it to suppress the pain he still felt from his injuries. He made more films but with his drug addiction beginning to spiral out of control he died in 1922 at the age of 31. The great tragedy for Reid is that he was recklessly given copious amounts of morphine in an era when drug rehabilitation was nowhere near as professional or widespread as it would later become.

Eddie Mannix worked at Metro-Goldwyn-Mayer from 1924 to 1962 and became notorious as a 'fixer'. Mannix was like the Winston Wolf of MGM. He was there to clean up the mess. Mannix is alleged to have arranged abortions, kept Judy Garland addicted to pills, and even killed George Reeves for having an affair with his wife. He resorted to blackmail on occasion to keep stars in line and was even on the scene before the police when it came to Hollywood deaths. Mannix was the general manager at MGM and enjoyed almost unlimited influence at the studio. It was Mannix who made sure gossip columnists didn't know a star was in rehab, covered up fights and car crashes, and fed false stories to the magazines to throw them off the trail of scandals. Mannix is even alleged to have had a hand in the death of Thelma Todd and the character assassination of Patricia Douglas after she claimed she was raped at a studio function. Mannix died in 1963.

The 1956 John Wayne film The Conqueror was shot in Utah near an area where nuclear weapons testing had taken place in the 1950s. The director Dick Powell died of cancer several years later and the two lead actors John Wayne and Pedro Armendáriz also developed cancer. Nearly half of the cast and crew later developed cancer and nearly fifty of them died. It is unavoidably speculated then that the cast and crew were working in an area that still had dangerous traces of radiation fallout.

Lucille Ricksen was a silent era actress who was born in 1910 in Chicago. She became a child model at the age of four and was on the stage by the age of five. Her full name was Ingeborg Myrtle Elisabeth Ericksen and she was the child of Swedish immigrants. The Hollywood studio bosses clearly didn't think that Ingeborg was much of a name for a rising star so they changed it to Lucille. You could describe her as a child star (Lucille Ricksen was only fourteen when she died in 1925) but the strange thing about Ricksen is that she sometimes played adult roles. When she was put in adult clothes and make-up she resembled an adult more than a child onscreen so studios decided to use her this way. This is obviously something that seems wrong and distasteful today. It is also deeply troubling that Ricksen had to pose for risque photo shoots to promote herself and her films.

The studio pretended that Lucille was sixteen to mitigate any bad publicity about their use of her. Alarmingly, it is said that Lucille had an affair with Charlie Chaplin's thirty-eight year-old brother Syd and even had an abortion. Both the Chaplin brothers would be in prison and registered sex offenders if they were around today. They both liked young girls. There were definitely some dark and weird things about the early eras of Hollywood.

Lucille Ricksen is a very early example of a bankable child star who was exploited by both her family and the studio purely for financial gain. Lucille was definitely the family cash cow. She was the only one bringing in any money so they all relied on her. This meant she had to constantly work and wasn't allowed to have a normal childhood. Her friends were all adults from the film industry so it was a very strange sort of childhood. Lucille was deprived the chance to just be a normal kid. She was exhausted in the end and appears increasingly fragile and ill in her movies. In just five years from 1920 to 1925 she made made around thirty-five movies and short films. That was a punishing ordeal for one so young.

The studio had taken to putting lipstick on Lucille and making her eyes darker so she could play adult roles. The strange thing about this is that her family didn't seem to object. I suppose they just wanted the money. In the 1924 film Rendezvous, thirteen year-old Lucille played the love interest of Conrad Nagel - who was forty years-old. They even have kissing scenes in the film. The makers of this film would be arrested today. Lucille was made to sign numerous contracts so the chance of a break from acting was impossible. She always had commitments to fufil. When you factor in the fact that Lucille had to travel a lot to promote the films and make personal appearances you can see how punishing this must have been in the end for a girl who was barely a teenager.

Lucille Ricksen died in 1925 of Tuberculosis and was suffering from malnutrition at the time. Ricksen really needed a long rest, medical care, and a more normal childhood but, sadly, she was chewed up and spat out by the Hollywood machine and greedy parents. She was bedridden near the end and slipped into a coma. In 1924 she made ten films in seven months. Lucille Ricksen was ill and exhausted and her body simply couldn't take any more.

The actress Marilyn Monroe, probably the most famous female sex symbol of all time, died in 1962 at the age of 36 from an apparent overdose of sleeping pills. There are of course though numerous theories about her death and many believe she was murdered. It has been alleged that Monroe was under CIA surveillance due to her intimate knowledge of the Kennedy brothers and alleged links to communists (which presumably stemmed from her marriage to the left-wing writer Arthur Miller). In his book Marilyn At Rainbow's End, Darwin Porter claims that Monroe was killed by the Mob. Darwin believes that Mafia boss Sam Giancana had Marilyn killed - possibly at the behest of one of the Kennedy brothers. The book claims that five Mafia enforcers used chloroform on Marilyn and then administered drugs to make it look like an overdose or suicide.

Theories on Marilyn's premature death continue to abound and probably always will. The mob story even includes an allegation that Marilyn's little black book detailing her sexual encounters with famous people was stolen during the murder to protect their identities. Jack Lemmon said it was completely true that Marilyn Monroe had an affair with JFK. "One day I was coming back home and there's this helicopter doing a low lazy circle above it. And there were these guys in funny suits and funny glasses, standing around watching Marilyn Monroe and JFK having a frolic in the pool. So whatever stories you've heard about Marilyn, that one is true: it was a big affair for her and she was in a deep relationship with JFK. Whether he thought the same, we'll never know. I think for sure she shouldn't have got mixed up in the Kennedy clan. But she was the type of girl that looked straight into trouble and no one could ever advise her."

Despite her fame it seems that Marilyn was not the most popular person in Hollywood. The director Billy Wilder found the unreliability and persistent lateness of Marilyn Monroe so annoying and unprofessional that when his famous movie Some Like It Hot finished shooting he didn't bother to invite Monroe to the wrap party. Tony Curtis added to the general sense of irritation Monroe seemed to have created on the set by saying that kissing Monroe in the film had been like kissing Hitler. Eddie Fisher once said of Marilyn - "Marilyn Monroe was a serious player. She used people — she played them off, and I was a victim, too. When I first met her at the start of the Fifties, she made a beeline for me and asked me out on many occasions for a date. But she wasn't the 'Marilyn' creation then — pretty, yes, but fake. And that was the problem." The real truth is that we simply don't know in Marilyn was murdered or simply died an unhappy death thanks to an overdose (which may or may not have been intentional). It's a mystery that seems destined to be the subject of many more books for years to come.

Millicent Lilian "Peg" Entwistle was born on February the 5th, 1908, and grew up in Wales and London. She moved to the United States as a young woman and became a stage actress on Broadway. She was blonde haired and attractive (she looks a bit like Kisten Dunst in some of her photos) and appeared on the stage with the likes of Ethel Barrymore and Humphrey Bogart (who were obviously rising actors at the time and not yet famous). Peg Entwistle soon began to make waves on the stage and earned a lot of acclaim for her performances. No lesser figure than Bette Davis is said to have become a fan after watching Entwistle on the stage. Now that she had made her mark on the stage, Peg now targeted the next obvious rung up the ladder - movies. She dreamed of becoming a film star and appeared to have all the necessary attributes to do so.

Peg Entwistle landed her first (and sadly last) film role in a 1932 thriller called Thirteen Women. She was only in a supporting role but it was a break and foot in the door nonetheless. Peg had high hopes for the film and a movie career but she was dismayed when most of her supporting role in Thirteen Women ended up on the cutting room floor. Entwistle's role originally amounted to about twenty minutes of screen time (which was fairly major in an hour long film) but in the final version - after editing - Peg Entwistle was upset to see that she was only in the film for about four minutes.

The extensive cuts were made after the film scored low marks with preview audiences. Peg was pretty devastated because it seemed that preview audiences and the editor patently didn't want to see more of her character in the film. Her performance evidently hadn't made much of an impression at all. After the disappointing experience of Thirteen Women, Peg Entwistle found her dreams of Hollywood success had evaporated in swift and cruel fashion. She was offered no more film work and ran out of money. She couldn't even afford to get out of Hollywood and go back to New York where she'd enjoyed success on the stage. Peg felt friendless and alone. She felt like she had hit rock bottom.

Peg Entwistle decided to end her life. She did this in dramatic and bizarre fashion. Entwistle climbed up to the top of the famous Hollywood sign in the hills of Los Angeles and jumped from the letter H. She apparently used a ladder to get up there although where this ladder came from is something of a mystery. At the time the sign read Hollywoodland rather than Hollywood. It was all academic anyway. Peg was determined to jump and go out in the most theatrical way possible.

Why she chose such a bizarre death is open to question. It could be that Peg's less than subtle intended subtext was designed to declare that Hollywood had killed her by destroying her dreams. A hiker found her body. Peg had died as a result of multiple fractures from the fall. She was 24 years-old. It is possible that she may have been alive for some time after the fall and in agony. It definitely wasn't the most logical way to end it all. Peg left a suicide note which read - "I am afraid I am a coward. I am sorry for everything. If I had done this a long time ago it would have saved a lot of pain."

There was a rather tragic coda to Peg's death because one day after her suicide, a letter was delivered to Peg's apartment from the Beverly Hills Playhouse offering her a part in a new play. Had this letter arrived one day earlier she probably wouldn't have killed herself. The death of Peg Entwistle earned big headlines in the media because of the theatrical and

strange nature of her death. Given her desire to be a famous
actress, it was darkly ironic that Peg became much more
famous in death than she had been in life.

Trivia - Peg's ghost is said to haunt the area near the
Hollywood sign. Several people have reported encountering it
over the years.

Jean Seberg became famous in 1956 when Otto Preminger
chose her out of 18,000 hopefuls to play Joan of Arc in the
1956 film Saint Joan. Seberg, who was from Iowa, was only
seventeen. Although her performance in Saint Joan was
unfairly panned she had the last laugh on her critics by
becoming a stylish icon through her role in Jean-Luc Godard's
Breathless. Seberg was most famous for her short hair. To this
day if a female celebrity has a short haircut it is sometimes
referred to as a Jean Seberg crop. Her other film roles
included Paint Your Wagon and The Mouse That Roared with
Peter Sellers. Seberg was hip and gamine. She was definitely
an icon although more appreciated in Europe than Hollywood.
Seberg didn't seem too phased by this and was happy to live in
France and make European movies.

Seberg's political views, which included some public support
for the Black Panthers, drew the attention of the FBI and their
treatment of her was scandalous. The Black Panthers were a
revolutionary leftist organisation formed in 1966. The crazy
thing about this affair is that all Seberg had done was donate
some money to the Black Panthers to support a scheme they
had to supply free meals to children in deprived areas. It
wasn't as if she was advocating a revolution or taking up arms.
She was just trying to help poor kids get a square meal! They
say though that no good deed goes unpunished and so it was
with Jean Seberg.

Crazy old J Edgar Hoover declared that Seberg must be
"neutralized" and so the FBI launched a nasty and shameless
smear campaign against her. They put Seberg under
surveillance (which made her paranoid) and spread a fake

newspaper rumour that father of her impending baby was not her French husband but a Black Panther leader. The FBI memo read - 'The possible publication of Seberg's plight could cause her embarrassment and serve to cheapen her image with the general public'.

Seberg suffered a miscarriage and her mental health declined. She killed herself in 1979 in Paris. She proved that her dead baby was white (thus debunking the Panther story) and sued three publications but the FBI badgered her until she went back to France. Seberg was only forty years-old when she was found dead in her car with mineral water and barbiturates on the seat beside her. She had been missing for ten days when she was found.

Seberg was clearly someone who battled depression but it wouldn't be an overstatement to say that the FBI played a big part in her sadly premature death. When she stayed in a New York hotel once she discreetly put sticky tape on some of the drawers and wardrobes and - sure enough - when she returned found the tape had been disturbed and her stuff rifled through. When Seberg gave an autograph to a fan in the street one time, FBI men searched the girl afterwards and tried to find out what Seberg had said.

At the time of Seberg's death there were stories that someone else might have been present when she died (which would obviously suggest possible foul play) but Seberg's husband (who later committed suicide himself himself) said that she had tried to take her life before several times. Seberg's last brush with Hollywood was in the 1970 film Airport (which starred Burt Lancaster and Dean Martin). After this she mostly made increasingly experimental European films.

In 2014, Ben Urwand wrote a book in which he claimed that Hollywood studios, in order to maintain their access to the German market in the 1930s, financed German weapons and even aborted a plan to make a film about Jewish mistreatment in Germany because the Nazis complained. It should be noted that other film historians have refuted Urwin's claims. They point out that many studio executives were Jewish themselves and actively involved in anti-Nazi groups. Walt Disney personally hosted Nazi filmmaker Leni Riefenstahl when she came to Hollywood promote her film Olympia in 1938. Riefenstahl directed the famous Nazi propaganda film Triumph of the Will. Despite gossip that Disney was a Nazi sympathiser, Walt Disney's studio did produce anti-German propaganda films as part of the war effort so these claims seem vague at best.

George Reeves played Superman in the first live action film based the comic book character and also when the character moved to television for the popular Adventures of Superman in the 1950s. Reeves wore a corset to keep his stomach in and had an awful woollen costume that irritated his skin. He had to suffer for his art to play the Man of Steel. Reeves once knocked himself out smashing through a door that he wrongly presumed was a prop. Reeves was forced to make personal appearances as Superman and he loathed this. Because the children really did think Reeves was Superman, the actor was subject to all manner of dangers.

A boy once stabbed him with a compass and another pulled a gun on him and said he wanted to know if the bullets would bounce off Superman's chest. Reeves had to persuade the boy to put the gun down by saying it would be dangerous if the bullets bounced off his chest into the crowd. Reeves was found dead in his bedroom at the age of 45 from a gunshot wound while the show was still in production in 1959. The verdict was suicide (the motive was alleged to be the fact that Reeves was frustrated by the way his acting career had turned out) but many suspect he was murdered. Reeves was said to be having an affair with the wife of infamous Hollywood fixer Eddie Mannix. The unavoidable speculation is that Mannix had Reeves killed.

If you believe Scotty Bowers and his book about his time as a sexual hustler in Old Hollywood, Katherine Hepburn was a

lesbian with an active sex life. 'Katharine Hepburn and I would
become the very best of friends. In the course of time I would
fix her up with over 150 different women. Most of them she
would only see once or twice, and tire of them immediately.
But there was one exception. There was a very cute little 17-
year-old trick that I set Kate up with early in our friendship.
The girl's name was Barbara. Shortly after they started seeing
one another Kate bought Barbara a brand new two-toned Ford
Fairlane as a gift. Kate saw Barbara off and on for just over 49
years. Three months before dear Kate passed away in June
2003 Barbara received a letter from Kate's attorneys. With the
letter was a check for $100,000.'

Thelma Todd was a blonde actress known as Hot Toddy and
The Ice Cream Blonde who famously appeared in the Marx
Brothers films Horse Feathers and Monkey Business. Her last
film was The Bohemian Girl with Laurel & Hardy. She
appeared in 120 shorts and movies and was an infamous girl
around town known for a fast lifestyle and colourful love life.
Todd made a fantastic foil for Groucho Marx and was a pretty
accomplished performer. She was sort of like the Marilyn
Monroe of her day with her blonde pin-up girl looks. Todd was
a former Miss Massachusetts on the pageant circuit but in real
life she was not your stereotypical dim blonde bimbo at all and
had once attended a teacher training college. Todd was spotted
by Hollywood talent scouts though and so instead of becoming
a teacher she headed for Hollywood and became an actress.

Todd owned an eatery in Malibu called Thelma Todd's
Sidewalk Cafe and it became a popular place for celebrities
and hipsters of the era to hang out. She had got into the
restaurant business because she didn't plan to be an actress
forever. Thelma knew her looks would fade in the end and the
studios would inevitably replace her with someone younger so
she wanted to have something else to do when that time came.
In 1935, at the age of 29, Todd was found dead behind the
wheel of a car in her garage. The garage belonged to her
business partner and occasional lover Roland West. Todd and
West actually lived in an apartment above the eatery. Believe it

or not, West's estranged wife Jewel Carmen lived there. It was West and Carmen who started the business in the first place.

The official verdict on Thelma Todd's death was carbon monoxide poisoning and it was presumed that this was either suicide or an accident. However, some movie historians and people at the time believe that Todd might have been murdered. Blood was found on her mouth and a second autopsy did not happen because her body was cremated. The Chicago Tribune claimed that Thelma Todd was found with two cracked ribs and a broken nose. If this was the case then it seems unlikely to have been a simple case of suicide. Todd could hardly had done these injuries to herself. Even if she fell forward or sideways in the car after she passed it's hard to see how these serious injuries could have happened.

The day after Todd's death a newspaper published an article in which it suggested foul play and revealed that Todd had been the victim of extortion threats demanding money. Who the extortion threats came from was not stipulated and presumably unknown (obviously, an extortionist is unlikely to sign their name on a threatening letter). Suspects in Todd's death include Pat DiCicco, who was Todd's ex-husband. He had Mob links and was known to have been violent to Todd in the past. Pat DiCicco is said to have felt betrayed and humiliated when Todd left him so he had a motive.

The mobster Lucky Luciano is also a suspect. Luciano had a relationship with Todd that was said to be stormy and obstreperous. It is said that Luciano wanted Todd to open a casino in her restaurant but she had dug her heels in and refused to do this. As you might imagine, this didn't make him very happy. Hollywood gossip suggested that Luciano had got Todd hooked on drugs and was determined to maintain influence over her. A Mob boss would patently be capable of having Todd killed and making it look like a suicide so Lucky Luciano was an obvious suspect in this suspicious death.

Jewel Carmen is also sometimes dubbed a suspect. Carmen

apparently threatened Todd a few times because she was angry that the restaurant wasn't making much money. Carmen probably wasn't too thrilled either to see that her estranged husband was attracted to Todd. The alleged motive for Carmen is presumably jealousy more than anything. Roland West is also a suspect in Todd's death although - in mitigation - his grief seemed genuine enough when her body was found. The motive in this theory is that West was jealous of Todd's numerous affairs and boyfriends.

Believe it or not, Thelma Todd's mother Alice is even a suspect. Alice Todd was the main financial beneficiary of Thelma's early death. Alice Todd had began preparations to build herself a house before Thelma died despite having no visible means to fund such a project. Thelma's death naturally gave Alice the financial means to build her house. This is what you might describe as a convenient and rather suspicious turn of events.

One thing that goes against this theory though is that Alice was pretty vocal at the time in declaring that her daughter had been murdered. If she had murdered Thelma you'd think she'd want to go along with the suicide theory to cover her tracks - unless it was all a cunning double bluff. Alice Todd seems like a longshot wen it comes to potential murder suspects. She probably would have been the least likely to have done this (if indeed it was even a murder in the first place).

One theory concerning Todd's death is that she had accidentally locked herself out after a night on the town and decided to sit in her car in the garage to keep warm and somehow accidentally killed herself by putting the engine on. The day she died, Thelma had been late getting home from a party and had been dropped off around 3am. The counter to this argument is that people in this era were warned a lot about carbon monoxide poisoning with cars and Thelma was pretty intelligent and so would have been aware of these dangers herself. It could be though that her logic that night was clouded by alcohol.

One factor which counters the suicide theory is that Todd was apparently very happy at the time of her death. There was no sign of depression or unhappiness. Thelma died during production of the 1936 Laurel & Hardy film The Bohemian Girl. Most of Todd's scenes in the movie were cut by the producer Hal Roach after her death but as a tribute one scene of her singing Heart of a Gypsy was kept intact.

SCANDAL

Harvey Weinstein is thankfully behind bars at last. The powerful Hollywood producer abused his power with sexual assaults on dozens of famous women in the film industry. The shocking thing about the Weinstein case is that he got away with it for so long. The list of women who Weinstein abused is long and extensive. Asia Argento said that Weinstein raped her in New York when she was 21. Argento said that did not struggle because she was feaful that her career might be ruined if she resisted. Gwyneth Paltrow said that when she was 22 she was asked to meet Weinstein in his hotel room and fled in terror when he asked for a massage.

Rosanna Arquette said that after Pulp Fiction she went to Weinstein's hotel room to pick up a script and he appeared in a towel and tried to put her hand on his groin. She spurned his advances and believes that her career suffered as a result. Heather Graham said that Weinstein told her she would have to sleep with him to get a part in a film. She declined to do this and didn't get the part. Mia Sorvino, Eva Green, Cara Delevingne and Léa Seydoux all said that they had to fight off Weinstein after he made unsolicited sexual advances.

Lysette Anthony said she was raped by Harvey Weinstein in the late 1980s. Angie Everhart said that Weinstein masturbated in front of her on a boat during the Venice film festival. Erika Rosenbaum said that Weinstein masturbated behind her while holding her neck. Daryl Hannah said Weinstein was a nightmare when she made Kill Bill and kept trying to get into her hotel room and grope her breasts. Ashley Judd said that when she was twenty years-old, she was asked to go to Weinstein's hotel room where he tried to get her to watch him taking a shower.

Annabella Sciorra said that Weinstein raped and sexually harassed her. Salma Hayek said that Weinstein once threatened to have her killed when she rejected his sexual advances. When she was a young actress in the 1990s, Angelina Jolie said she had to fight off Weinstein in a hotel room. She vowed never to work with him again and never did. The screenwriter Louisette Geiss said that Weinstein masturbated in front of her while she was making a pitch. Lupita Nyong'o said that Weinstein repeatedly told her that he could advance her career if she had sex with him. Lena Headey, Katherine Kendall, and Claire Forlani are among many, many others who have also spoken about frightening encounters with Weinstein.

Louis CK was once one of the most feted comedians in Hollywood. He had his own TV show and was about to release a new movie. His stand-up shows were highly acclaimed and lucrative. However, whispers about his conduct began to circulate in gossip columns and tittle tattle sites. The rumours were that Louis CK had a compulsive habit of masturbating in front of women - even if they hadn't consented to this. His victims included staff and female comedians he met at shows. At first, he tried to evade the allegations and imply they were not true. They were however completely true. In November 2017, Louis CK confessed to his sexual misconduct in a statement.

Not so long ago, Bill Cosby was making plans for a Netflix special to celebrate his fifty+ years in showbusiness. Cosby was an inspiration to comedians like Jerry Seinfeld and a philanthropist and elder statesman of the black community. Cosby broke colour barriers in the sixties show I Spy and in the 1980s created one of the most popular sitcoms of the decade in The Cosby Show. Cosby was also always much sought after for commercials. You would struggle to find a more trusted figure in American public life than Bill Cosby. Cosby had a very dark secret though that his money and influence had somehow always been able to keep hidden.

Cosby was a serial rapist who sedated numerous women with the sedative methaqualone (Quaaludes). There were always dark rumours about Cosby and he had been interviewed by the police in the past but no action was ever taken against him. This changed when the comedian Hannibal Burgess called Cosby a rapist during his act. This provoked scrutiny into Cosby's past and private life and very soon women were emerging to allege that Cosby had sedated and sexually abused them.

The sexual abuse and rapes by Cosby dated back to the 1960s. A staggering fifty women soon came forward with similar stories about Cosby. While the statute of limitations made action in all of these cases impossible, Cosby's 2004 sexual assault of Andrea Constand was used as the main basis to convict Cosby. On April 26, 2018, Cosby was found guilty of all three counts against Constand. On September 25, 2018, he was sentenced to 3–10 years in state prison. Cosby has shown no remorse for his crimes or ever admitted any guilt - despite the overwhelming evidence against him.

Christopher Savino created the Nickelodeon animated series The Loud House. He was another Hollywood figure caught up in sexual abuse allegations. There were several complaints against Savino. One of the complaints involved a woman who was developing an animated project under the mentorship of Savino. Savino began to send her lewd texts and make sexual advances and suggestions and when she rejected his advances he pulled the plug on her project. This was a disgraceful abuse of his power. His contract with Nickelodeon was axed and he had to offer an apology.

Stephen Collins is best known for his roles in Star Trek: The Motion Picture and the TV show 7th Heaven. It later transpired that from 1973 to 1994 he indecently exposed himself to three young girls who were aged from ten to thirteen. Strangely, the revelations came from the leak of a confidential marriage therapy session Collins had with his (then) wife Faye Grant. Collins claimed Grant used the leak for ammunition in a divorce. Collins evaded any charges for his sexual misconduct. April Price, who was only thirteen when

Collins exposed himself to her, said that Collins lied when he said he had only exposed himself to her once. She said he did it on three occasions. These days, Stephen Collins lives in Iowa away from the limelight and is married to a 7th Heaven superfan.

The Casting Couch was all too real in Old Hollywood and many industry figures abused their positions of power and influence to exploit aspiring stars. Harvy Weinstein was by no means the first person in Hollywood to use his power to his own grubby ends. 'Hollywood producer Darryl F. Zanuck was legendary in the industry — but not just for the movies he made,' wrote the NY Post. 'Zanuck worked his way through actresses on the sofa in his office faster than the credits rolled on his flicks, according to the tome "The Zanucks of Hollywood: The Dark Legacy of an American Dynasty" by Marlys Harris.

'His daily bedding of budding starlets operated like clockwork. At 4 p.m. every day, his Fox Century City studio would shut down while Zanuck shuttled a young woman through a subterranean passage to his green-paneled office, according to Harris and Deadline Hollywood. "Anyone at the studio knew of the afternoon trysts," Harris wrote. "He was not serious about any of the women. To him they were merely pleasurable breaks in the day — like polo, lunch and practical jokes." In 1937, Zanuck won the Academy of Motion Picture Arts and Sciences' first prestigious Thalberg award for producing. It was the same decade that Variety first used the now-ubiquitous term for the abuse of power that Zanuck and other Hollywood execs were perpetuating behind the scenes — "the casting couch," according to Slate.'

The film director Roman Polanski is an infamous and controversial figure because of an incident that happened in 1977 when he was 43 years-old. Polanski took a thirteen year-old aspiring model named Samantha Gailey to a house in Hollywood and gave her a Quaalude. He then had sex with Gailey despite her protests and told her afterwards not to say anything about their encounter. Gailey told her mother though and Polanski was arrested. As part of a plea-bargain to protect Gailey from a public trial, Polanksi's charges were dropped except for statutory rape.

In 1978, while this criminal case was still ongoing, Polanski fled from the United States and went to Europe - eventually ending up in France. Polanski has not returned to the United States since 1978 for good reason. He would be arrested if he ever set foot on American soil again. There is still an international arrest warrant out on Polanski and he was once detained in Switzerland but it seems that he has largely got away with his crime. The strange thing about Polanski is that he has continued to make many films in Europe with some of the biggest stars in Hollywood. For some unknown reason, cancel culture never seemed to target Roman Polanski.

In 1975, a ten year-old Brooke Shields was booked by her mother to have some photographs taken by New York City photographer Garry Gross. Brooke Shields' mother was paid $450 for her daughter's photography session. The controversy came when some of the photographs featured a partially naked Brooke Shields. When she was seventeen, Brooke Shields took legal action to try and block Gary Gross from marketing or selling the photographs taken of her when she was ten. Surprisingly though, the legal action was not successful. The judge ruled that Gross could continue to sell the photographs so long as he didn't sell them to 'pornographic magazines or publications whose appeal is of a predominately prurient nature.'

Max Landis is the son of the famous (or infamous if you prefer) film director John Landis. Max Landis carved out a very promising career as a writer in Hollywood. He wrote Chronicle, American Ultra, Victor Frankenstein, and Bright. He also wrote comic books and has directed and produced. A colourful motormouth sort of character, Landis was also a popular guest to interview. However, his career was brought to a juddering halt in the wake of the Weinstein scandal when a number of women came forward to make sexual abuse allegations against him. Anna Akana, a co-worker of Landis, accused him of sexual assault and called Landis a psychopath who sexually abused and assaulted women.

MAD Magazine editor Allie Goertz said that Max Landis was notorious for being a sleazeball and Landis' former girlfriend Whitney Moore said he subjected her to horrific abuse. Eight women eventually came forward to accuse Landis of sexual abuse. Zoe Quinn, a video game developer, wrote on Twitter 'Sometimes men who commit sexual assault are talented screenwriters and their work comes with baggage. other times, they're Max Landis. I'm SO glad people are finding out what a piece of s*** he is.' Many of the women said Max Landis was violent and described incidents where he would choke them. Josh Trank, who directed Chronicle, said he banned Max Landis from the set of the film because he knew that Landis was a notorious slimeball.

Sondra Locke was most famous for being the former partner of Clint Eastwood. While they were together she frequently starred in his films. The relationship turned sour in the end though and the fall out was most unpleasant. In a memoir entitled The Good, the Bad, and the Very Ugly, Locke gave Eastwood both barrels and blasted him as best she could. What made Locke's book rather eccentric was that it featured her former husband (who happens to be gay) too. Locke insists in the book that he's psychic and has strange powers!

Locke claimed that Eastwood persuaded her to have two abortions and a tubal ligation under false pretences, sabotaged her directorial career after they split up, and secretly fathered two children with another woman during the last three years of their relationship. Sondra Locke filed a palimony lawsuit against him in 1989 after he changed the locks on their Bel-Air home and had her possessions placed in storage. Locke dropped the suit in 1990 in exchange for a development-directing pact at Warner Bros. According to Locke, the deal was a sham and she discovered that Eastwood was compensating the studio to keep her out of work by rejecting any and all projects she pitched.

In 1995, Locke sued Eastwood a second time, for fraud and breach of fiduciary duty. "It just wasn't true," said Eastwood. "I wasn't in collusion with Warner Bros to keep her out of work. I can't say let's take a lie-detector test because the law doesn't adhere to that, but I would in a second." "How could I really win against Clint?" Locke wrote in her memoir. "No one else ever had. What I didn't know was that I would wage my fight against him virtually alone. Those friends who had urged me forward would disappear." In 1996, just minutes before a jury was to render a verdict in Locke's favour, the two parties agreed to settle for an undisclosed amount.

William Taylor was a very successful director in Old Hollywood but his death is a mystery that has yet to be solved. He was said to be one of the first advocates of what is known as the casting couch. If you wanted to be in one of his films you had a better chance if you slept with him. He also liked young girls and didn't care if they were of legal age. Taylor was found dead in his office but one knows who murdered him. It could be that it was a relative of one of the young starlets he took advantage of. Legend has it that the police removed evidence of Taylor's contacts and liaisons to spare studio blushes. He was known to have connections to crime figures so this added another potential line of inquiry into his murder. We simply don't know who killed him though.

The most famous Old Hollywood scandal came in 1921. The comedian 'Fatty' Arbuckle held a party in his hotel suite and a woman there named Virginia Rappé fell ill, dying four days later from peritonitis. Arkbuckle was arrested and charged with manslaughter with lurid stories swirling around that he'd assaulted the woman and was some sex crazed monster in real life. He was in fact completely innocent and acquitted in six minutes at the final trial. Hollywood was reluctant to put Arbuckle's name on anything afterwards officially but he did direct films under an assumed name and work with Chaplin and Keaton again and many others who stood by him. He was eventually offered a three film contract by a studio and died a happy - and innocent - man. Many accounts of Arbuckle disregard the fact that he was cleared of any charges and received an apology from both the courts and the film industry before he died.

The Twilight Zone is one of the most famous and iconic shows in American television history. The show ended in 1964 and its creator Rod Serling died in 1975. In the early 1980s, Steven Spielberg decided to make a big screen anthology version of The Twilight Zone and hired Joe Dante and George Miller to direct segments. The other two segments would be directed by Spielberg and his friend John Landis. Thanks to films like Animal House and An American Werewolf in London, Landis was one of the hottest young directors in Hollywood. Spielberg and Landis were such good friends that Spielberg even made a cameo in The Blues Brothers for Landis. The Twilight Zone movie was something of a vanity project for Landis and Spielberg and they couldn't wait to get started.

Spielberg planned to direct a remake of The Monsters Are Due On Maple Street for the movie while Dante and Miller were also assigned classic TV episodes to update. Landis, eager to outdo the others, decided to come up with an original story called Time Out. The story was about a racist who must experience persecution at the sharp end when he is sent back in time. Landis cast an actor called Vic Morrow as the lead of Time Out. Morrow was quite well known (especially for the TV show Combat!) but his career was in the doldrums by 1982. John Landis was a brash and arrogant director who could be demanding of his crew. Landis was determined that Time Out would be the most spectacular segment in the movie and this had tragic consequences.

During a sequence set in war torn Vietnam, Vic Morrow was required to carry two child extras across a river as explosions went off around them and a helicopter loomed overhead. Morrow and the child extras should not have been doing this dangerous stunt. As the helicopter hovered into the shot, Landis kept shouting for the helicopter to get lower. Tragedy struck when the rotor blade was hit by debris and the pilot lost control. The chopper violently and suddenly lurched into the river and landed right on top of Morrow and the child actors. The children were killed instantly and Morrow was decapitated by the rotor blade. It later transpired that the hiring of the child actors for a night shoot violated child labour laws. Steven Spielberg was sickened by the accident and very angry.

Bizarrely, the film was not scrapped though. Spielberg adapted the whimsical and gentle Kick the Can so that he could complete his contribution to the film in a matter of days. The friendship between Spielberg and Landis was over. Landis resumed his career with decent success at first but by the 1990s was pretty washed up. He never fufilled his potential. A manslaughter trial somehow absolved Landis of blame in the accident. Landis came off as arrogant and unsympathetic during the trial. He tried to pass the blame off to special effects people. The recklessness and arrogance of Landis had put Morrow and the children in danger in the first place and that is something that Landis will always have to live with.

Lana Turner was once involved in a real life drama that was as outlandish and dark as anything in a Hollywood movie. 'Lana Turner was known as a Hollywood femme fatale on screen, and that role extended into her real life as well,' wrote Vintag. 'In 1958, Turner's boyfriend, mobster Johnny Stompanato, was found stabbed to death in her home. Stompanato was a reputed associate of mobster Micky Cohen. He had been stabbed in the abdomen with a butcher knife, and during the ensuing investigation, Turner's 14-year-old daughter confessed that she was the one who delivered the fatal blows. Cheryl Crane said that she stabbed him to protect her mother, who she felt was in danger from Stompanato. At the inquest, Turner took the stand and described Stompanato as hyper-possessive and prone to fits of rage. She said that she had told her daughter of her plans to end the relationship that night, saying, "I'm going to end it with him tonight, Baby. It's going to be a rough night. Are you prepared for it?"

'Turner said that Stompanato flew into a rage when she told him it was over. She said, "He grabbed me by the arms and started shaking me and cursing me very badly, and saying ... that if he said jump, I would jump; if he said hop, I would hop, and I would have to do anything and everything he told me or he'd cut my face or cripple me. And if ... when it went beyond that, he would kill me and my daughter and my mother." "I was walking toward the bedroom door and he was right behind me, and I opened it and my daughter came in. I swear it was so fast, I ... I truthfully thought she had hit him in the stomach. The best I can remember, they came together and they parted. I still never saw a blade." The jury returned a verdict of justifiable homicide, but rumors swirled that Turner had been the one to wield the blade and simply had her daughter take the blame. Although many continue to believe that, her daughter seemed to settle the question in her 1988 autobiography where she again admitted stabbing Stompanato, who she said was sexually abusing her.'

Gwyneth Paltrow said that when she was starting out in Hollywood as a teenager, she attended an audition where the casting director suggested they finish the audition process in his bedroom. She left immediately and was completely shocked. The casting director obviously chose who to give the part to on whether or not they slept with him. Geena Davis said that in one of her early auditions as a young actress she was asked to perform a lapdance. She had no idea at the time that this was out of the ordinary and sleazy. The disgraced Harvey Weinstein was, as we have noted, someone who notoriously exploited the audition process to his own sleazy ends. Weinstein would ask aspiring actresses to come to his hotel room to discuss a part and - of course - when they got there it would simply be Weinstein alone. He would often appear with just a towel on and pretend he had just got out of the shower.

Anthony Edwards said that when he was fourteen he was sexually abused by Gary Goddard. Goddard is the founder of an entertainment design firm and has been accused of sexual abuse by several people in Hollywood. Goddard was a close associate of the director Bryan Singer - who has also been accused of numerous sexual abuse incidents. Martin Weiss was a Hollywood manager who both Disney and Nickelodeon used to find child actors for their shows. Weiss was convicted of sexually abusing client Evan Henzi over thirty times when Henzi was only eleven and twelve years-old. Weiss entered a no-contest plea to two counts of committing lewd acts on a child under the age of 14.

For most of his career, Kevin Spacey seemed to have a charmed life. He was one of the most acclaimed screen actors in the world and always much in demand. His love of the theatre saw him work extensively on the stage and become the director of the Old Vic in London's West End. He had four million Twitter followers and was a frequent presence on chat shows where his quick wit and knack for impressions made him a popular guest. However, in 2017, the enviable life of Kevin Spacey imploded to the point where he has become an outcast in Hollywood. It all started when the actor Anthony Rapp claimed that Spacey had made a sexual advance to him when he was fourteen years-old.

Spacey took to Twitter to address the allegation and did so in such a clumsy fashion that he only made the situation worse. Spacey said he had no memory of the incident (Spacey was apparently drunk at a party at the time) and was horrified at learning of it, claiming he would reflect on his conduct. What really made things worse though was that Spacey chose this statement to finally come out as a gay man. It seemed grossly insensitive. Not only did Spacey make it seem as if he was trying to deflect from the actual issue at hand (Rapp's allegation of inappropriate conduct against a minor) it also had a rather unfortunate subtext in the apparent conflation of homosexuality and sexual misconduct with minors. A number of gay celebrities felt it was crass of Spacey to use this statement to come out. Things though were about to get a whole lot worse for Spacey. In all (at the time of writing) fifteen men have come forward with allegations of sexual misconduct against the former darling of stage and screen.

TELEVISION

Jaimee Foxworth became famous as a child actor playing Judy Winslow on the TV sitcom Family Matters. When her time on the show ended she was plunged into the familiar problems that many former child stars face. Her money began to run out and she couldn't get acting work. It was later revealed that Foxworth had spent two years (from 2000 to 2002) making porn films under the name Crave. "It was, to me, the quickest money," she said. "I was so naïve, and I was drinking. I couldn't hold my head high. I couldn't walk around and say, 'My name is Jaimee Foxworth' without someone saying, 'Ew,' or, 'We heard about you'. That's the most degrading part. I lost all my confidence. I lost all my self-esteem. I lost friends. I lost some family members. When I was on Family Matters, I thought the money was never going to stop. I thought I was never going to be broke. So I say to young girls, always have another option. Try to go for your dreams. Don't try to be just what you scc on TV."

The Golden Girls was one of the most popular sitcoms of the 1980s. Although the characters in the show were firm friends, the same could not be said for all of the cast. The most difficult relationship seemed to be between Bea Arthur and Betty White. For reasons which no one ever seemed able to pinpoint, Bea Arthur despised Betty White and once referred to her as a c***. It is said that when shooting the show in front of a live audience, Bea Arthur was very detached and liked to get completely into character whereas Betty White was very informal and would crack jokes with the audience. This is said to have driven Bea Arthur mad. For her part, Betty White said that she knew that Bea Arthur disliked her but she could never fathom the reason for this.

Another popular show that had to cope with actors who didn't get on is Sex and the City. It is a very open secret that Kim Cattrall loathes Sarah Jessica Parker. A third Sex and the City movie was abandoned when Cattrall declined to return. The source of this feud is speculated to stem from Parker becoming an executive producer on the show in the second season. This producer role meant that Parker got a pay rise. Parker's increased salary is said to have irked the other cast members - most notably Cattrall. Another alleged source of the feud is that during an Atlantic City location shoot for the show, Sarah Jessica Parker rented a house for herself, Kristin Davis and Cynthia Nixon. Kim Cattrall was left to find her own house. It is generally alleged then that Cattrall felt alienated by the clique that the other three actresses created for themselves.

At the 2004 Emmy Awards, Kim Cattrall pointedly sat at a separate table to her Sex and the City co-stars. In 2008, Parker said "Honestly, we are all friends and I wish I saw more of Kim. She mentioned money and no one should vilify her for it. People made a decision that we had vilified her." Cattrall returned for the two spin-off movies but was said to not be on speaking terms with Parker during production of Sex and the City 2. In 2017, Cattrall confirmed that she would not return for Sex and the City 3 and said she had never been friends with her co-stars. Cattrall then aimed a dig at Sarah Jessica Parker - "This is really where I take to task the people from Sex and the City, and specifically Sarah Jessica Parker. I think she could've been nicer. I really think she could've been nicer. I don't know what her issue is."

The feud between Kim Cattrall and Sarah Jessica Parker escalated in 2018, when Parker offered condolences to Cattrall for the death of her brother. In response, Cattrall took to Instagram, where she wrote - 'When will that @sarahjessicaparker, that hypocrite, leave you alone?' Your continuous reaching out is a painful reminder of how cruel you really were then and now. Let me make this VERY clear. (If I haven't already) You are not my family. You are not my friend. So I'm writing to tell you one last time to stop exploiting our tragedy in order to restore your 'nice girl' persona."

Parker and her co-stars were bemused by the spite of Cattrall's response. In 2018, Parker said "I'd just like to remind everybody that there is no catfight. I have never uttered an unkind, unsupportive, unfriendly word, so I would love to redefine it. I also want to remind everybody that there were four women on the set and I spent equal time with all of them, so this was not a set with two women who didn't get along. I've always held Kim's work in high regard and always appreciative of her contributions. If she chooses not to do the third movie, there's not a lot I can do to change her mind and we must respect it. That's the only thing I've ever said about it, you know?"

The popular TV show Little House on the Prairie was shot on land purchased in Simi Valley Ranch. The land came at a bargain price because an experimental sodium cooled nuclear reactor operated by the Rocketdyne Corporation had previously released a huge wave of radioactivity in the area. Although the land was deemed safe to shoot Little House on the Prairie, it is open to question as to whether or not this was actually the case. Five members of the cast later died from cancer - most famously Michael Landon. Landon was only 54 when he died of pancreatic cancer. Patrick Swayze, who had connections to Simi Valley, also died of pancreatic cancer at a young age.

The Waltons is a much loved TV series about a family in rural Virginia during the Great Depression and World War II. It was created by Earl Hamner Jr and ran from 1972 to 1981. There were several TV movies after the show ended. The Waltons is the ultimate comfort blanket television. The series started life as a TV movie called The Homecoming: A Christmas Story. Ellen Corby and the children played the same roles as they later did in the TV show but Patricia Neal played Olivia, Edgar Bergen played Grandpa, and Andrew Duggan played Grandpa. These last three actors were replaced in the TV show. Walton's Mountain, though supposed to be in Virginia, was actually the mountain range just across from the Warner Bros Studios in Los Angeles.

Ralph Waite, who played John Walton Sr, was an alcoholic when the show started. Playing John Walton encouraged him to get sober. Waite felt that there was no way he could play such a clean cut role model on television when his real life was a mess. Will Geer, who played Grandpa Walton, was married twice but openly bisexual. Geer was involved in gay and left-wing activism and in the 1930s and in a relationship with homosexual activist Harry Hay. Geer was blacklisted in the early 1950s for refusing to testify before the House Committee on Un-American Activities. When Geer died in 1978 it was a great blow to the show as Grandpa Walton was such a beloved character.

Ellen Corby, who played Grandma, was gay in real life (although she was married when she was young for ten years) and, believe it or not, a teacher in transcendental meditation. When she suffered a stroke in 1976 that affected her ability to speak it was written into the show. Richard Thomas, who played John Boy, left after six seasons although a hoped for movie career never quite transpired. Thomas seemed to make a lot of TV movies where he was cast as a villain - writers obviously liking to twist his goody-goody John Boy image. Thomas returned to the role of John Boy for the second Waltons TV movie and stayed for the others that followed. Thomas remains a busy TV and stage actor.

When Richard Thomas left the show, the producers recast the part of John Boy and Robert Wightman played the character in seasons eight and nine. It seems as if Wightman was never quite accepted as 'substitute John Boy' though and the character became more of a background figure. Wightman played John Boy in the first TV movie but was then dumped so Richard Thomas could come back. Wightman is conspicuous by his absence whenever they have a Waltons reunion or retrospective. Wightman has continued to work since The Waltons although in relative obscurity. You might have seen him in the horror film Stepfather III.

None of the other Waltons children managed to quite carve

out a completely successful acting career. Judy Norton Taylor, who played Mary Ellen Walton, posed for Playboy in 1985 to try and shake off her Waltons typecasting. Today she runs a chain of dinner theaters with her husband. She's acted in a few bits and pieces, including Stargate. Jon Walmsley, who played the musical Jason Walton, was born in England and the voice of Christopher Robin for Disney's Winnie the Pooh cartoons. Walmsley is a real life musician and has mostly worked as a composer since The Waltons ended.

Eric Scott, who played Ben Walton, now runs a parcel delivery service, while Kami Cotler, who played the red haired youngest Walton child Elizabeth, became a teacher. Mary Elizabeth McDonough, who played Erin Walton, appeared in more acting jobs than the other children and guest starred in shows like The West Wing and ER. McDonough later wrote a memoir about her time on The Waltons. Michael Learned, who played Olivia Walton, said her career was at 'rock bottom' before she was cast in the show. Like Ralph Waite, she suffered from drinking problems but says she has been sober since 1977. David W. Harper, who played the likeable mechanical minded Jim Bob Walton, last acted in the 1985 Chevy Chase film Fletch. He seems to be a private person who doesn't do many interviews but he has supported the many Waltons reunions.

Desperate Housewives star Nicollette Sheridan sued ABC when her contract was terminated. She also accused the show's creator Marc Cherry of hitting her on the head. Cherry said he gave her a light tap to demonstrate a scene she had to pay. The subsequent court cases did not reach a verdict in Sheridan's favour. What did come to light in the evidence though was the fact that Teri Hatcher was not very popular on the set. Sheridan said that Hatcher was the meanest actor she had ever worked with. Sheridan was none too popular either. In his evidence, Marc Cherry said that co-stars Eva Longoria and Felicity Huffman both expressed relief and happiness when they heard that Sheridan had been axed from the show.

The popular nineties sitcom The Fresh Prince of Bel-Air was a rather troubled production in its early years thanks mainly to Janet Hubert-Whitten, who played Vivian Banks. Hubert-Whitten was described as 'overbearing' on the set and constantly demanding more lines. What made things even worse though was the fact that Hubert-Whitten absolutely despised the show's star Will Smith and made no secret of this. When the producers had to do something to clear the tension the solution was obvious. The show obviously couldn't go on without Will Smith but Hubert-Whitten was expendable and so they replaced her with Daphne Maxwell Reid. Years later, when asked if she would liked to have a reunion with her Fresh Prince co-stars and bury the hatchet, Hubert-Whitten merely snorted and called Will Smith an asshole.

seaQuest DSV was a sci-fi show launched in 1993 by NBC. A vague sort of cross between Star Trek and Voyage to the Bottom of the Sea, the show revolved around the 'seaQuest DSV' - a high-tech submarine and deep submergence vehicle operated by the United Earth Oceans Organization (UEO), a global coalition of up-world countries and undersea confederations, similar to the United Nations. The show was produced by Amblin and so had the participation of Steven Spielberg. Big things were expected of seaQuest DSV and a considerable amount of money was spent on it. However, it only ran to three seasons and proved to be something of a misfire in the end. The ratings started strong but quickly plummeted and there were so many changes from season to season that the show could never really establish any sort of identity or a consistent tone.

Roy Scheider was persuaded to head up the cast of seaQuest DSV as Captain Nathan Bridger but Scheider quickly tired of the show. He made no secret of the fact that he thought it was awful. "It's total, total childish trash," Scheider told the press while shooting season two. "I'm ashamed of it. I feel betrayed. I feel I've not been told the truth. We were going to present human beings who had a life on land as well as on the boat. We've had one script that has done that. The other shows are Saturday afternoon 4 o'clock junk for children. Just junk - old, tired, time-warp robot crap. It's not even good fantasy. I mean Star Trek does this stuff much better than we can do it. To me the show is now 21 Jump Street meets Star Dreck. I don't do this kind of stuff. I said (to the production executives), 'If I wanted to do the fourth generation of Star Trek, I would have signed up for it. I wouldn't have done seaQuest. You guys have changed it from handball into field hockey and never even bothered to talk to me.'"

The show's problems were compounded by moving production from Los Angeles to Orlando for the second season. Several members of the cast promptly left because they didn't want to relocate to Florida. The departing cast members included notable lead players like Stephanie Beacham and Stacy Haiduk. Roy Scheider decided that it was high time for him to escape from this sinking ship too and he begged NBC to release him from his contract. They agreed but only on condition that he make a few guest appearances as Bridger in season three. Scheider was replaced by Michael Ironside as Captain Oliver Hudson in the show's final season.

Edward Kerr, who joined the cast in season two as Lieutenant James Brody, begged the producers to kill him off in season three (of which they obliged). Kerr thought that seaQuest DSV was so bad that it might harm his career if he stayed part of it! Other casting additions to season two were Michael DeLuise and Peter DeLuise, which, if nothing else, proved that their father Dom knew how to pull a few strings! In 1996, after thirteen episodes of season three had been broadcast, NBC pulled the plug on seaQuest DSV.

What had started with much fanfare and promise had quickly become a rather forgettable show. Not a terrible one but just something that didn't really engage or stick in the memory. seaQuest DSV just never really clicked with audiences. One expected much more of something from the Amblin stable but - ultimately - seaQuest DSV could never quite work out what sort of show it wanted to be. All the behind the scenes problems (and the ever changing cast) were obviously not much help either. seaQuest DSV was a very big deal when it was launched but these days feels somewhat forgotten. It never became a cult show or developed the sort of fandom enjoyed by other sci-fi shows of yesteryear.

Gary Coleman was a familiar face on television from 1978 to 1986 thanks to his role as Arnold Jackson in the sitcom NBC Diff'rent Strokes. The show was about two African-American boys from Harlem taken in by a rich white Park Avenue businessman and widower named Phillip Drummond (Conrad Bain). Coleman's famous catchphrase in the show ("Whatchu talkin' 'bout Willis?") was much imitated by seventies and eighties kids. The show seemed be something of a curse for its three main young leads - Coleman, Todd Bridges (who played Arnold's brother), and Dana Plato (who played Phillip's daughter Kimberly). Coleman, Bridges, and Plato found it nigh on impossible to get acting work after Diff'rent Strokes and were all beset with numerous personal troubles. Bridges is the only one of the trio who is still alive - which is pretty amazing when you take into account his own highly troubled history with drug addiction.

Gary Coleman had nephritis - a kidney disease which stunted his growth and made him still look like a child even when he became a mature adult. He could probably have played Arnold Jackson for decades without appearing to age much - though it obviously didn't come to that in the end and Coleman probably would have considered that a fate worse than death. Although the show was very popular, Coleman never cared for Diff'rent Strokes much himself and couldn't wait for it to end. He thought Diff'rent Strokes was dull and conservative and grew to dislike the long working days spent shooting the show. Diff'rent Strokes was notorious for special episodes where a social issue (like drug abuse, alcoholism, racism, and even child sexual abuse) would be explored. Gary Coleman really hated the preachy 'issue of the day' tone of Diff'rent Strokes.

There were a lot of famous guest stars in Diff'rent Strokes. Muhammad Ali appeared in one episode and Nancy Reagan (who fronted the Just Say No drugs campaign) was in the anti-drugs episode. In hindsight that was pretty ironic because in real life Todd Bridges and Dana Plato both went on to take enough drugs to sedate a herd of elephants. As for Gary Coleman's festering dislike of the show, he especially hated the fact that he had to play the same character - a smartass kid - for several years. By the end of Diff'rent Strokes, Coleman had grown to loathe Arnold Jackson.

Legend has it that by the end of Diff'rent Strokes, Coleman would sometimes refuse to say Arnold's famous catchphrase because he was so sick of it. Coleman was eighteen years-old by the time Diff'rent Strokes came to an and resented the fact that the production team still treated him like a little kid. In mitigation though he still LOOKED like a little kid so maybe they just forgot sometimes that he had grown up. In 1989, three years after the end of Diff'rent Strokes, Coleman had to sue his parents and business manager for dipping into his earnings and trust fund. Coleman had made $50,000 an episode on Diff'rent Strokes from the age of thirteen so this trust fund was a sizeable nest egg. He never spoke to his parents again after the legal case. The successful legal action netted him $1,280,000.

Gary Coleman, like many child stars, found that adult life in the entertainment industry - and ordinary life in general - was no bed of roses. His acting career was effectively finished as soon as he became an adult. No one wanted to hire a 4'8 actor who still looked like a chubby child. Coleman was hopelessly typecast as Arnold Jackson but that was the sort of role he was too old to play now. By 1999, Coleman had blown his money and was working as a security guard after being declared bankrupt.

Gary Coleman was clearly not a happy man. He was famously bad tempered and once punched a woman who asked him for an autograph. He required regular dialysis treatments and his health declined. He married a young woman named Shannon Price near the end of his life but it was a rather fractious marriage it seems with many fights and arguments. Gary Coleman suffered an epidural hematoma after a fall in 2010 and died at the age of 42. By the end of his life he was reduced to comic cameos or eighties nostalgia talking head shows. It was a far cry from the late seventies and early eighties when he was one of the most recognisable faces in America. It seems that Gary Coleman didn't cope very well with the immense fame that came his way at an early age. The rest of his life was plainly a struggle. This all seemed to leave him embittered and angry.

Dana Plato shot to fame at the age of 13 when she won a part in Diff'rent Strokes. Plato had to choose between an ice-skating career and acting and, all things considered, she probably should have stuck with the ice-skating. Plato played Kimberley in Diff'rent Strokes. Prior to this she had small parts in Exorcist II: The Heretic, Return to Boggy Creek, California Suite, and The Six Million Dollar Man. Believe it or not though it was Plato's appearance on The Gong Show (which was a crazy talent competition) which apparently attracted the attention of the producers of Diff'rent Strokes.

Dana Plato, who had wholesome girl next door looks (Plato looks a bit like a young Chelsea Clinton in some of her photographs), looked set for a long career in Hollywood but this didn't turn out to be the case at all. Plato was booted off of Diff'rent Strokes for getting pregnant (her character Kimberley was supposed to be younger than Plato and the producers simply didn't want a teen pregnancy storyline in the show - which was odd because they usually loved shoehorning social issues into Diff'rent Strokes!) and her career went nowhere fast - thanks in large part to her drug problems.

Plato returned to Diff'rent Strokes for some guest appearances but after it ended in 1986, Dana found that her telephone rarely seemed to ring anymore. Her acting CV became a barren desert with the occasional wind blown tumbleweed. In the tradition of numerous other washed-up former child stars she was reduced to doing cheapie straight to video type movies that hardly anyone watched. Dana was rather like Erin Moran in this respect. It must be pretty rough to come out of a big TV show and then find that literally no one wants to hire you anymore.

After a supporting role in a forgotten 1989 film with the highly original title Prime Suspect (an interesting cast for this one - it featured Doug McClure, Frank Stallone, and Michael Parks!) 1992 saw Dana lend her voice to the video game Night Trap and star in something called Bikini Beach Race with the now disgraced porn actor Ron Jeremy. Other long forgotten Plato trash classics included Lethal Cowboy and martial arts obscurity Blood Boxer. In 1995, Plato tried to cash in on her long lost sitcom fame by starring in the softcore lesbian drama Different Strokes: The Story of Jack and Jill...and Jill. Literally no one saw any of these movies Dana was making. She was trapped in the Phantom Zone of Straight to Video Hollywood invisibility.

Dana lost custody of her son and even had breast augmentation in the hope of becoming a Playboy model. The nadir for Plato came in 1992 when she was arrested for trying to rob a video store with a plastic gun. It was a pretty bizarre story and for this reason made the headlines in the United States. This was literally the first time Dana had experienced any fame since Diff'rent Strokes ended but - alas - it was for all the wrong reasons. This eccentric robbery only netted Plato a paltry $160. She was clearly a woman who needed help. Dana was sentenced to five years probation for the robbery but weeks later got into more trouble when she was arrested for forging a valium prescription. This landed her in jail for thirty days.

Sadly, you probably didn't need to be Nostradamus to predict that Dana Plato wouldn't make old bones. She was found dead in her RV home in 1999. The verdict was an overdose of painkillers and other medication. She was just 34 years old. The money and fame she once enjoyed was merely a distant memory by the time of her sad death. Dana's former mother-in-law was reported to claim that Dana had been murdered. Her finger of suspicion was aimed at Dana's fiance Robert Menchaca.

A sleazeball promoter named Shane Bugbee had tried to cash in on Dana's death by putting a CD and booklet about her up for sale which was tastelessly titled Dana's Last Breath. It was said to include a photo of her dead body - which only Menchaca could have taken because he was there when she died. Whatever the truth it was all rather morbid and distasteful. There was a very tragic coda to this story because Dana's son Tyler committed suicide eleven years after her death at the age of 25.

When Gary Coleman paid his tribute to Dana he said that she was a wonderful woman but it was a blessing in disguise she had died because this meant there was now no chance of a Diff'rent Strokes reunion. Stay classy Gary! The fanciful chances of a Diff'rent Strokes reunion were obviously reduced to zero when Coleman died himself. This left Todd Bridges as literally the only cast member of Diff'rent Strokes still alive. He played Willis Jackson in the show and was a successful child actor even before this big break.

Bridges found life after Diff'rent Strokes difficult and has been arrested for numerous drugs convictions. In 1989 he was charged with the murder of a Los Angeles drug dealer but was found not guilty of the charges after it was proven that he was somewhere else at the time. Despite his troubles, Bridges has managed to keep working (mostly TV movies) and these days lectures youngsters about the perils of drugs. Todd Bridges, despite his troubles, turned out to be the most stable and wise of the kids in the show.

Jamie Lynn Spears created a scandal when she became pregnant at the age of 16 while appearing in Nickelodeon's Zoey 101. The scandal was trickiest for her eighteen year-old boyfriend Casey Aldridge. He could have easily received statutory rape charges for having sex with someone who was underage. He pled guilty to a misdemeanor. The actor Charlie Heaton (who plays Jonathan Byers) couldn't attend the premiere for Stranger Things 2 because trace amounts of cocaine were reportedly found in his luggage at LAX. Heaton was sent on a plane back to Europe. However, he was not arrested or ever charged with anything and believes the faint drug traces found on him were a result of recently attending a party. The incident with Charlie Heaton had no consequences for the actor nor his career and he returned for Stranger Things 3.

In 2018 a man named Charlie Kessler took legal action against the Duffer Brothers. Kessler had made a short Camp Hero inspired film called Montauk in 2011 and said that the Duffers based Stranger Things on his ideas without giving him any credit. Kessler claimed he had pitched a show based on the Montauk conspiracy theories to the Duffers at the 2014 Tribeca Film Festival party. The Duffers dismissed the claims as baseless and without merit. A court case was later arranged in 2019 to settle the matter but Kessler withdrew his claims before the case even began. The Duffers had produced private emails proving that they were already discussing (what would eventually become) Stranger Things as far back as 2010. The Duffers were adamant that they had never seen Kessler's short film nor discussed anything with him. Kessler was forced to admit that he was mistaken to claim that he had somehow influenced Stranger Things.

In 2020, there was another attempt to claim that the Duffers had stolen the idea for Stranger Things when Irish Rover Entertainment announced they were going to sue over their claim that the idea for Stranger Things was inspired by Totem - a screenplay by Jeffrey Kennedy (who is an actor and writer with minimal credits to his name). The lawsuit stated that Totem was about a girl with supernatural powers who must help her friends find a portal gate to an alternative universe that is supernatural in origin. The lawsuit claimed that Stranger Things had stolen the plot, mood, setting (Indiana), and even the characters from Totem. Irish Rover

Entertainment further claimed that Aaron Sims had worked on developing Totem and then took all of these ideas with him when he later worked on Stranger Things.

Netflix countered the new threat of legal action by saying that Jeffrey Kennedy had been peddling these conspiracy theories for years and that the Duffer Brothers had never heard of Mr Kennedy nor any screenplay called Totem. Netflix further accused Mr Kennedy of trying to secure money from Netflix for his 'baseless' claims. It seems highly unlikely that Kennedy's lawsuit will have any more success than that of Charles Kessler. It is of course fairly ludicrous to try and sue the Duffer Brothers for them having a similar idea to one of your own - especially when the similar idea in question is something that has been a constant staple of science fiction escapism for many decades. It would be like trying to sue the makers of Independence Day by saying that in 1976 you wrote a script about an alien invasion!

Chris Farley was born in Chicago, Illinois, in 1964. He was a comic performer and actor best known for appearing on Saturday Night Live from 1990 to 1996. Farley then made the switch to movies and appeared in films like Tommy Boy, Black Sheep, and Beverley Hills Ninja. At the time of his death he was preparing to be the main voice actor in Shrek. Farley had to be replaced by Mike Myers when he passed away.

Farley's hero was John Belushi. It was Belushi who had inspired Farley to get into comedy and become a performer. Sadly though he emulated Belushi all too well - both of these comic performers dying far too young thanks to drugs. Belushi became a star through Saturday Night Live and then moved into films with National Lampoon's Animal House and then The Blues Brothers with his friend Dan Akroyd. He had huge problems with drugs though and died in 1982 after a huge binge that ended with a 'speedball' of cocaine and heroin. At the time of Belushi's death, Akroyd had been writing Ghostbusters as a vehicle for himself and Belushi - the late Belushi eventually replaced by Bill Murray in the film.

Farley died on December the 17th, 1997. He was famously overweight so not the healthiest person in the world to start with. Added to this were his battles with drink and drugs. It was probably inevitable that without drastic changes to his lifestyle Chris Farley was never going to make old bones. At the time of his death, Farley was in Chicago. He had purchased an apartment in the John Hancock Building. This is an iconic tower in Chicago which was used in the movie Poltergeist III. Farley lived on the 60th floor. Farley had hooked up with a prostitute named Heidi and was in the midst of an epic and ultimately fatal and destructive drugs bender. He hadn't slept for days.

Farley had gone to Heidi's apartment at one point but then they ended up back in his place. He used crack and heroin during this prolonged and deadly binge. In the end Heidi became frustrated that Farley hadn't given her any money and left. Farley was lying on the floor in a sorry state when she departed. You'd probably have grounds to suggest that Heidi shouldn't have left Farley alone in such a terrible mess but she'd clearly had enough by this point. Maybe she just assumed he would sleep it off and wake up none the worse for wear. She probably wasn't thinking that straight herself after all the drink and drugs.

Farley's brother found Chris the next morning. He was wearing only pyjama bottoms and was inert. There was foam and liquid coming from his mouth. An ambulance was called but it was too late. Chris Farley was pronounced dead. He was 33 years-old - the exact age that John Belushi had been when he died from a drugs binge. Farley's cause of death was cited as morphine and cocaine intoxication. There were opened bottles of booze and prescription drugs all around the apartment. One obviously presumes that the authorities also found illegal narcotics.

It is doubtful that anyone could have survived the drugs bender that Chris Farley had undertaken. Farley's last completed movie was Almost Heroes. Sadly this film turned out to be a dud and was a rare case of Christopher Guest making a bad picture. It was released posthumously. Chris Farley had been to rehab many times but sadly was never able to stick at it long enough to get clean and sober. His poor health had become increasingly apparent in some of his last public appearances on television. He was bigger than ever and seemed hoarse and tired. There was a sweaty desperation to Farley's last performances. It was clear that he was struggling to summon forth his usual manic energy.

Farley's funeral was a star studded event full of famous faces from the world of comedy. Farley's friend and comedy partner David Spade was notably absent though - which led to speculation the pair had fallen out before Farley died. Spade later said though that he didn't go because he simply couldn't face it. He was too distraught. Chris Farley's remains were interred at Resurrection Cemetery in Madison. At the time of his death he had many film projects in the pipeline. If he had managed to conquer his demons and get healthy he could have been a much bigger star. Farley will always be remembered though for his stint on Saturday Night Live.

Thomas Gibson played Agent Aaron Hotchner for nearly a dozen seasons on Criminal Minds but then, to the shock of fans, seemed to be axed from the show. The reason why he left was because he kicked writer and producer Virgil Williams after a blazing argument during production of an episode (that Gibson was actually directing). "We were shooting a scene late one night when I went to Virgil and told him there was a line that I thought contradicted an earlier line," said Gibson. "He said, 'Sorry, it's necessary, and I absolutely have to have it.' He came into that room and started coming towards me. As he brushed past me, my foot came up and tapped him on the leg. If I hadn't moved, he would have run into me. We had some choice words, for which I apologized the next day, and that was it. It was over. We shot the scene, I went home – and I never got to go back."

The comedian Tim Allen became famous thanks to the sitcom

Home Improvement. Before he became famous, Allen spent time in prison for dealing drugs. He was arrested for possession of nearly a pound-and-a-half of cocaine at the Kalamazoo/Battle Creek International airport in Michigan in 1978. Allen spent 28 months in prison. He could have got a life sentence but managed to avoid this by revealing the names of other drug offenders he was involved with. Allen has always been honest about his past mistakes and the drugs bust never really harmed his career.

Rodney Alcala, a brutal serial killer active in the 1960s and 1970s, appeared as a contestant on the TV show The Dating Game. Alcala (born Rodrigo Jacques Alcala Buquor) was born in San Antonio, Texas, in 1943. Alcala is retrospectively chilling because of his relative success in society. He went to college, appeared on television, worked as a photographer, and got employment in a summer camp. He was hiding in plain sight all the time. He briefly served in the US Army as a clerk when he was young and didn't last very long. Rodney Alcala then raped and nearly killed an eight year-old girl named Tali Shapiro in California in 1968. Alcala fled from California and, with the help of a fake identity (he was now calling himself John Berger), he made his way to New York and enrolled in the film school at NYU.

Alcala killed in 1971 when he murdered a flight attendant in New York. This necessitated another swift departure and he gained a counselling job at a New Hampshire arts camp for children. By now though, Alcala's likeness was on FBI Wanted posters for the attack on Tali Shapiro and some of the kids at the summer camp where he worked reported him to the authorities when they noticed the similarities. He was arrested and taken back to California but fortune was on his side because the family of Tali Shapiro felt it was would be too distressing for the girl to testify in court against him. As a consequence he got a relatively light sentence and was given parole after less than two years in prison.

Alcala sexually abused a thirteen year-old girl upon his release but - unbelievably - he was then released AGAIN after another short spell in prison. This time, he went back to New York where he got a job as a typesetter and became a freelance photographer. The photography was something of a ruse. Alcala would pretend he was a hotshot fashion and art photographer. He would lure girls for a photography session and then murder them. The police later found hundreds of photographs of these girls but finding the bodies and remains was another matter entirely. Rodney Alcala was very adept at leaving no forensic evidence.

Among his known victims was Ellen Jane Hover - the goddaughter of Dean Martin and Sammy Davis Jr. In 1978, Alcala famously appeared as a contestant on the TV show The Dating Game. Alcala was introduced by the host as a successful photographer who enjoys skydiving. He was competing with two other male bachelors to win a date with the female contestant through answers they gave to her questions from behind a screen. Alcala was chosen but the woman found him so creepy when the screen was removed that she refused to go on the date. Alcala had long hair and was sort of good looking but there was definitely something of the night about him. He gave off creepy vibes.

After his brush with television fame, Alcala continued to kill but his luck finally ran out a few years later. Rodney Alcala was captured because he lured a teenage girl named Robin Samsoe from a beach. The girl's friends helped the police to construct an artist's impression of the abductor and this drawing was seen by Alcala's parole officer.

In 1980, Alcala was tried and sentenced to death for Samsoe's murder. From this point on a bizarre and laborious set of legal wrangles kicked in. The first conviction was overturned by the California Supreme Court because it was judged that the jurors did have sufficient information about the defendant. In 1986, Alcala was sentenced to death again but a Ninth Circuit Court of Appeals panel quashed this verdict.

The third trial of Rodney Alcala was a strange spectacle because he insisted on acting as his own attorney. Alcala was predictably eccentric and at sea in this task. He played a clip from The Dating Game, played songs, and - in a bizarre moment - even tried to question himself by putting on silly voices. Tali Shapiro, the girl he had attacked in 1968, bravely testified this time and Alcula was sentenced to death for a third time. He's 78 years-old now and still in prison. The thousands of photographs he took are still being studied by the police to see if they can identify who these people were and how many of them might have been victims.

One salient reason why Rodney Alcala went undetected for so long was that he moved around a lot. There were sometimes large geographical spaces between his victims and this obviously made it much more difficult to establish any pattern. He was a very evil and very dangerous man. Naturally, he tends to now be dubbed The Dating Game Killer in true crime profiles. Strange but true - One of the contestants on The Dating Game with Rodney Alcala later appeared in the sitcom Seinfeld.

Charlie Rose is one of the most famous talk show hosts in America. He also co-anchored CBS This Morning from 2012 to 2017. However, the urbane and respected image of Rose was dented when eight women accused him of sexual harassment in the workplace. Rose was accused of groping, making unwanted advances, and walking around naked. In a statement, Rose said - "In my 45 years in journalism, I have prided myself on being an advocate for the careers of the women with whom I have worked. Though I do not believe that all of these allegations are accurate. I always felt that I was pursuing shared feelings, even though I now realize I was mistaken." Bloomberg Television, PBS and CBS News all fired Rose in the end and things went from bad to worse for the veteran broadcaster when more women accused him of sexual misconduct - taking the total tally to seventeen.

Erin Moran shot to fame at the age of 13 as Joanie

Cunningham in the sitcom Happy Days. She even appeared in the spin-off show Joanie Loves Chachi before returning to Happy Days for its final run of episodes in 1984. When the show ended though, Erin Moran discovered life in Hollywood for former child stars can be a very unforgiving and cold hearted experience. The phone stopped ringing and she found it almost impossible to get any acting work. She also battled drug addiction and quickly blew through all the money she had earned on Happy Days. In 2011, Erin and some of her Happy Days co-stars sued CBS for money they believed was owed to them from profits and merchandise. Erin received just $65,000 in the settlement. In 2017, at the age of 56, Erin Moran died after being diagnosed with squamous cell carcinoma. She had been living in a trailer park and had run out of money. Moran's life had been a sobering journey from immense fame and success to poverty and obscurity.

Ariana Grande was famous at a young age thanks to the Nickelodeon sitcom Victorious. Ariana played a ditzy character called Cat Valentine. The show ran from 2010 to 2013 and revolved around a performing arts high school named Hollywood Arts High School. Ariana said that having to dye her hair red to play Cat left some lingering damage to her luxurious locks. TMZ alleged that Ariana had a stipulation in her contract on Victorious that none of her co-stars were allowed to have a bigger dressing room.

The lead actor in Victorious was Victoria Justice. Victoria was tipped to be a big star but flopped badly when she tried to become a singer. The huge success of Ariana Grande led to stories that Victoria and Ariana didn't get on and that Victoria was jealous of Ariana for having the musical career she was supposed to have. The stories of a rift between Victoria Justice and Ariana Grande were heightened when Ariana seemed to blame Victoria for the cancellation of Victorious. She wrote on social media at the time - "The only reason Victorious ended is because one girl didn't want to do it. She chose to do a solo tour instead of a cast tour. If we had done a cast tour Nickelodeon would have ordered another season of Victorious while Sam and Cat filmed simultaneously but she chose otherwise."

Victoria responded to Ariana apparently blaming her for the cancellation of Victorious by saying - "Some people would throw someone that they consider a friend under the bus just to make themselves look good. #StopBeingAPhony #IfTheyOnlyKnew." Many years after Victorious ended, an old clip of the cast being interviewed together surfaced on YouTube. In the clip, Victoria Justice seems to become annoyed when the other cast members say that Ariana is the best singer in the show. The rift between Victoria and Ariana seemed to be healed in August 2014 when they were both at the Nickelodeon Kids' Choice Awards and photographed together.

Victorious had a spin-off show called Sam & Cat - which Ariana also starred in. Sam & Cat teamed up characters from iCarly and Victorious. These were two of Nickelodeon's most popular shows but both had ended (hence Sam & Cat). Ariana Grande disliked acting and was only doing it as a springboard to a musical career. She couldn't wait to shed her ditzy Cat Valentine image. Victoria Justice isn't the only co-star who was alleged to have a fractious friendship with Ariana. There were many whispers that Ariana and her Sam & Cat co-star Jennette McCurdy had a difficult relationship.

Jennette McCurdy was alleged to have been unhappy that Ariana made more money than her on Sam & Cat. Ariana said that the story of her making more money on Sam & Cat was preposterous. "Jennette and I agreed upfront that we would be treated equally on this show in all regards (as we should be, considering we each work just as hard as the other on this show). The rumors circulating about our contracts and our salary not being equal are absolutely ridiculous and false. I don't know who's putting these idiotic quotes out there but I thought I'd straighten it out and try to end this nonsense. As far as the show goes, I don't know what's happening because I'm not directly involved with the problem but I just wanted to address this one rumor in particular because I am NOT making more money than my costar, nor do I think I should be. So we can all move on and get out of our heads that this was a money thing cause I don't play like that at all. I am, have always been and always will be about equality and fairness."

One of the (many) reasons why Sam & Cat was axed was that risque photos of McCurdy leaked online. Jennette McCurdy chose not renegotiate her contract in the end. When Sam & Cat ended, Ariana Grande thanked the crew on social media but did not refer to Jennette McCurdy. After Sam & Cat ended, Jennette McCurdy said of Ariana - 'We aren't better friends because being friends with you takes the "better" out of me. In fact, I might possibly be the worst version of myself when I'm around you. As for what happened to our friendship, it faded once through happenstance and it is happening this time through my stance. I'm standing up for myself. I'm not playing your games, letting you manipulate me, and succumbing to your twisted perception of reality.

'Where did I go? As far away from you as I can get. You won't be hearing from me anymore because sweetheart, being a friend to you was doing so much more for you than it was doing for me. You sucked the life right out of me, and I want my life back. ... So for these sincere reasons, I am officially dropping you as a friend. If I see you, I won't turn the other way and run (even though I want to). Instead, I'll just smile and end the conversation as quickly as possible, because no offense, but I don't want any of you rubbing off on me. Actually, that's pretty offensive. Oh well.' Jennette McCurdy later had a web series called What's Next for Sarah? The show (which is about a former child actress in Hollywood) featured a comic parody of Ariana called Gloriana. Jennette McCurdy now says that she texts Ariana and they are on much better terms these days.

In the early 1980s, two different business consortiums were interested in buying the Aladdin Hotel & Casino in Las Vegas. One group was led by the chat show host Johnny Carson and the other by the singer Wayne Newton. Carson's group decided to pull out of the deal and this allowed Newton's group to successfully acquire the casino. It apparently though rankled Carson a great deal that people thought that Newton had outsmarted him (which wasn't the case at all) and so Carson began to make Newton a figure of fun on his chat show and crack a number of jokes about the effeminate nature of the entertainer. This infuriated Newton so much that he confronted Carson and threatened to beat him up. As a consequence of this, jokes about Newton were dropped from Carson's show.

Paul Reubens is best known for his character Pee-Wee Herman - a childlike man who lives a whimsical and cartoonish existence. The character appeared in Tim Burton's film Pee-Wee's Big Adventure and Pee-Wee's Playhouse on television. In 1991, Reubens was arrested for indecent exposure in a porno cinema. Most people didn't even know what he looked like away from his Pee-Wee make-up so the sight of his mug shots were rather shocking at the time.

The fact that Reubens was in a porno cinema feels like a fairly tame sort of scandal from a modern perspective. This was a petty offence compared to the monstrous exploits of Cosby and Weinstein. However, at the time it was a very big deal, mainly down to the fact that Reubens was a kids TV star. Reubens had further trouble when the police seized his collection of vintage erotica on the grounds that it was child porn - something which Reubens adamantly denied. Reubens managed to survive the scandal and started working again. Many celebrities supported him and thought the police had been heavy handed in their treatment.

Cory Monteith was best known for his role as Finn Hudson on the Fox television series Glee. Monteith had appeared in many TV shows like Stargate Atlantis and Flash Gordon and his movie roles included Final Destination 3 and Deck the Halls. It was Glee though that made him a star. Despite his fame and success, Monteith had a troubled youth and battled drink and drugs problems. Sadly, his demons got the better of him in 2013. He was found dead in his room at the Fairmont Pacific Rim hotel in Vancouver. The inquest revealed that he had died of a heroin overdose. There was also codeine and morphine in his system and two empty bottles of champagne in his hotel room. Monteith had been trying to get clean and sober and it is speculated that, after a period of sobriety, his tolerance for drugs was low and so this binge proved fatal.

Patricia Arquette said that when she was cast as Allison DuBois in the TV show Medium, she had a fierce argument with one of the producers over her weight. The producer insisted that Arquette (who had just given birth in real life) should lose some weight to be more attractive in the show but Arquette stood her ground and refused to accept this demand. Arquette argued that Allison DuBois was a working mother with three kids so why on earth would she look like a pencil slim fashion model!

One Tree Hill was a TV show that ran from 2003 to 2012. It was a popular teen drama and very successful. However, behind the scenes, all was not well. A writer on the show named

Audrey Wauchope later said she had endured sexual harassment from One Tree Hill's showrunner Mark Schwahn. The actresses in the show later released a statement in which they confirmed Wauchope's allegations and offered their full support.

The original plan for the sitcom Friends was to have a more diverse cast to reflect the melting pot that is New York. The creators have conceded that the cast they went with doesn't reflect the cosmopolitan nature of New York. Sherri Shepherd, who played museum guide Rhonda, says she wasn't asked back after commenting on the lack of diversity in Friends. It has been speculated that Friends came about because Warner Bros wanted to turn the 1992 Cameron Crowe film Singles (which was about twentysomething friends in Seattle) into a

TV show but couldn't get permission. At one point, Cameron Crowe threatened legal action when he heard about Friends. He thought they were ripping off his film.

The main cast in Friends were paid $22,000 an episode when Friends began in 1994. By the end of Friends, the main cast were making one million dollars an episode. Co-creator Marta Kauffman said she thought it was ridiculous that the cast got one million dollars an episode in the last season. She felt this was an inflated salary. The salaries of the cast were upped from season to season. During the negotiations for the last pay rise, the Friends cast walked off the set in unison at one point. It was a move designed to display the solidarity of the actors. Brooke Shields said in her memoir that when she did a seductive scene with Matt LeBlanc as a guest star on Friends, her then boyfriend Andre Agassi was so enraged he smashed all of his tennis trophies.

You'll notice that Pottery Barn (an upscale home furnishing company) features in Friends. Warner Bros admitted that a deal with Pottery Barn was struck to mitigate the costs of the production of Friends. David Schwimmer says he snubbed the limelight for years after Friends ended because he found it difficult to adjust to being famous. Although Matthew Perry says he was never intoxicated on the set of Friends he admits that he was hungover at times. Perry says he finds it hard to watch the Friends episodes that were shot when he was battling his addiction to painkillers and alcohol. Paul Rudd said that when the finale wrapped and everyone was in tears he cracked a joke about what an amazing ride it had been (the joke being that Rudd was only in a handful of episodes) but no one laughed.

Jennifer Aniston almost lost out on Friends because she was starring in another sitcom called Muddling through. NBC deliberately put popular films up against Muddling Through to harm its ratings. They wanted it to be axed so that Jennifer Aniston would be available. The only spin-off from Friends was the sitcom Joey with Matt LeBlanc. The show had Joey moving to New York to try and kickstart his acting career. Joey was cancelled after two seasons because of poor ratings. The last episodes were never even broadcast. Matt LeBlanc felt that his failure to persuade Friends writer and co-creator David Crane to work on Joey was one of reasons why it didn't really work. LeBlanc said that, in hindsight, he should have refused to do Joey unless Crane was involved.

Kathleen Turner, who played Chandler's transgender father on Friends, says she wasn't made to feel very welcome by the cast. Turner said she would now turn down the part of Chandler's transgender father today because the role could be played by a real life transgender actor. The Friends reunion special apparently took eighteen months of negotiations before it was given a green light. Matthew Perry was the most difficult person to sign for the reunion.

Anissa Jones became famous as the blonde haired kid Buffy on the sitcom Family Affair. The show ran on CBS from 1966 to 1971. Jones was thirteen when Family Affair ended and, like many child actors, found that life after appearing in a successful TV show was difficult. She tested for the part played by Linda Blair in The Exorcist but the director William Friedkin felt that Jones was too associated with Family Affair to be believable in a different role. Jones was dismayed by the fact that she already seemed to be typecast and drifted away from acting. She began to shoplift and even worked in a Donut store. When she eighteen, Jones came into possession of the trust fund money that she she earned on Family Affair. This was a recipe for disaster as Jones had developed drug habits by now. In August 1976, Jones died after taking a cocktail of barbiturates, phencyclidine, cocaine and methaquaalone. She was just eighteen years-old.

David Carridine had a long and eclectic CV but is probably best known for the Kill Bill films and his role in the TV show Kung Fu. Carradine was a famously eccentric character whose life had included many bizarre incidents and drugs convictions. In 2009, the actor was 71 and shooting a new movie in Bangkok, Thailand. He was found dead in his hotel room closet hanging from a rope. Autoerotic asphyxiation was the obvious explanation for his death. This involves starving oneself of oxygen to heighten sexual pleasure. A surprising amount of people have allegedly died as a result of autoerotic asphyxiation. They include the singer Michael Hutchence, the British politician Stephen Milligan, and the musician and composer Kevin Gilbert. After his death, two of Carradine's former wives said that they weren't completely surprised by his strange death because his sexual interests had always been 'dark' and weird. There was a macabre and distasteful coda to this story when grisly photographs of Carradine's autopsied body began to appear online.

HOLLYWOOD AND RACE

Old Hollywood was not exactly famed for its treatment of black actors. They were usually consigned to supporting roles playing maids, bell-hops or servants. The best they could hope for was to be the comic relief or maybe play a musician. The Birth of a Nation, an epic 1915 film by D. W. Griffith, depicted black people as savages and the Ku Klux Klan as the heroes! It was black actors and filmmakers themselves who had to fight against these ingrained stereotypes and prejudices. Amazingly, up until fairly recent decades it was still deemed acceptable for white actors to black themselves up and play black or even Asian characters. This sort of thing was common in old films.

In the days of silent film and early talkies, there were 'race films' produced. These films were made with black crews and black casts and produced solely for black audiences. Most of these films were lost and (as they were not watched by white people) rather erased from history. It said something for the state of society and Hollywood that the only way a black actor could get a leading role was in a 'race film' made purely for a black audience.

Paul Robeson's rich voice (forever linked with the song Ol' Man River) saw him become the first African-American to play Othello on Broadway. He was a giant of the stage and between 1925 and 1961, Robeson also recorded and released some 276 songs. "In the early days of my carer as an actor," said Robeson, "I shared what was then the prevailing attitude of Negro performers — that the content and form of a play or a film scenario was of little importance to us. What mattered was was the opportunity, which came so seldom to our folks ... Later I came to understand that the Negro artist could not view the matter simply in terms of of his individual interests, and that he had a responsibility to his people who rightfully resented the traditional stereotyped portrayals of Negros on stage and screen."

Robeson was one of the first artists who refused to perform to
segregated audiences. Robeson was deeply interested in
politics and what was going on in the world and never afraid to
express his views. He was involved in the anti-imperialism
movement and visited Spain during the Civil War there
because he believed in the International Brigades's cause.
Robeson was a frequent visitor to the Soviet Union (where,
one might argue, Robeson displayed a naive admiration for the
Stalin brand of communism) in the 1930s and this later led to
his passport being taken away.

He was blacklisted in the McCarthy era and appeared before
the House of 'Un-American Activities' Committee. When he
was asked why he didn't just move to Russia, Robeson replied
- "Because my father was a slave, and my people died to build
this country, and I am going to stay right here and have a part
of it just like you." Robeson's political views harmed his career
in the United states and he found himself having to travel to
generate funds. His later years were blighted by ill health and
a nervous breakdown. Like many famous figures, Robeson was
more celebrated after his death than he sometimes was in life.

Hattie McDaniel was the first black actor in Hollywood to be
nominated and win an Oscar. This was for her role as the
servant Mammy in Gone With the Wind (a film that, to put it
mildly, rather whitewashed the issue of slavery). McDaniel was
not allowed to attend the premiere of the film in Atlanta
simply because she was black. At the Oscars she had to sit in a
special segregated area well away from her white co-stars.
When black actors appeared in a big film like Gone with the
Wind or Casablanca they were relegated to very minor roles in
which they were the supportive employee or servant to white
characters.

Sidney Poitier was the first African-American to win a Best
Actor award and the second African-American to win any
Oscar. This was a result of his performance in the 1963 film
Lilies of the Field. Poitier was the first black actor to gain
leading man status in Hollywood. Poitier said that in his early

days he would often turn up on the set of a film and be the only black person among the entire cast and crew. Sidney Poitier first made his mark in a 1950 film called No Way Out. He played a doctor who encounters racial prejudice. In the Heat of the Night, one of the films that made Sidney Poitier a star, was banned in some areas of the American south. "Up until then," said Poitier's co-star Rod Steiger, "you just didn't get that kind of exchange between black and white actors. The races in cinema, much as in real life, didn't mix."

Sidney Poitier became more of a director than an actor in the 1970s and took a long break from screen roles at one point. He said in his memoir that this was because he sensitive to suggestions in the black community that he was becoming typecast as the 'decent unthreatening black man' in movies. The 1982 comedy film Stir Crazy, directed by Sidney Poitier, was at the time the highest grossing film ever directed by a black director. This record was eventually beaten though when Scary Movie (directed by Keenen Ivory Wayans) outgrossed Stir Crazy twenty years later.

Ethel Waters was the first black actress to star in a TV sitcom. This was an ABC show called Beulah which ran in the early 1950s. Waters didn't last very long though. She quit the show because she felt it featured black stereotypes. Diahann Carroll was the first black actress to star in her own television series on American television. This was in the NBC sitcom Julia - which ran from 1968 to 1971. Julia was groundbreaking in that it was one of the first American television shows that avoided stereotypes when it came to black characters.

John Kitzmiller was the first black actor to win the Cannes Film Festival Award for Best Actor. This was for the 1957 film Valley of Peace. James Bond fans will know Kitzmiller best for his role as Quarrel in the first ever Bond film Dr No. Gail Fisher was the first African-American actress to have a speaking role in a television commercial. She is probably best known for 1970s television series Mannix (where she played Peggy Fair). She won two Golden Globes and an Emmy for her television work.

The Nat 'King' Cole Show, which made its debut on NBC in
1956, was the first television show to be hosted by a black
performer. Dorothy Dandridge was the first black actress
nominated for an Academy Award for Best Actress. This was
for the 1954 film Carmen Jones. Halle Berry was the first
African-American woman to win an Oscar for best actress in a
leading role. She won the Oscar for her performance in the
film Monster's Ball.

Eddie Murphy was the biggest box-office star in Hollywood for
much of the 1980s. One might argue that he was the first black
actor to attain this status. Murphy was a comedian who sprang
to fame on Saturday Night Live. He became a huge film star
thanks to pictures like Beverly Hills Cop, Trading Places, 48
Hours, and The Golden Child. Murphy's star began to dim in
the nineties and he was involved in a number of flops before
making a transition to more family oriented films. He has
though enjoyed some critical success and was nominated for
an Oscar for his role in Dreamgirls. Murphy is one of the ten
most profitable Hollywood actors of all time and proved
beyond doubt that black actors could be both the leading man
and the star name at the top of the poster.

Nichelle Nichols is forever immortal for her role as Nyota
Uhura in Star Trek. Uhura was the translator on the Starship
Enterprise and quite a groundbreaking character for a black
actress at the time. Nichols played this part in the original Star
Trek television series and also in six star Trek feature films.
Trivia - Nichelle Nichols was thinking about leaving Star Trek
at one point to do some Broadway plays but Martin Luthor
King Jr told her she should stay on Star Trek because Uhura
was a great role model for black children. Nichols took his
advice and stayed on the show.

Duane Jones was the first black actor to play the lead hero in a
horror film. This was in George Romero's classic 1968 film
Night of the Living Dead. Despite the racial subtext of the film,

Romero said Duane Jones was cast as the lead because he was the best affordable actor they knew and not because he was black. Duane Jones was later director of the Maguire Theater at the State University of New York at Old Westbury and the artistic director of the Richard Allen Center for Culture and Art in Manhattan.

Things might be getting better in Hollywood when it comes to diversity but we still have a long way to go. Nia Long believes she missed out on a part in the 2000 film Chalie's Angels because she was black. The part went to Lucy Liu in the end. Another black actress, Thandie Newton was also in contention to be one of the 'Angels' in the film but lost interest when she found the director McG unbelievably crude during the audition. Stacy Smith, founding director of the Media, Diversity and Social Change Initiative at USC's Annenberg School for Communication and Journalism, conducted a study which found that in modern day Hollywood only 28.3% of speaking characters with dialogue were from non-white racial/ethnic groups. Her study also found that only 33.5% of speaking characters were female.

WEIRD FACTS ABOUT OLD HOLLYWOOD

Tallulah Bankhead was known for going 'commando' and eschewing underwear. This became a problem on the set of the Alfred Hitchcock film Lifeboat when Bankhead's character had to climb a ladder. Members of the cast and crew complained and felt that Bankhead was going way too far in her exhibitionism.

The original Hollywood sign read Hollywoodland. It required 4000 light bulbs to illuminate it at night.

Jackie Coogan was one of the most popular child actors of Old Hollywood and appeared in films like The Kid, Oliver Twist, and Tom Sawyer. He is believed to have earned around four million dollars as a child actor. However, when Coogan turned twenty-one he tried to access his money and found that his parents had spent it all. Coogan took legal action against his stepfather and mother and although the money was gone the case did lead to what is known as the Coogan Act. This is a law which states that studios must set aside at least 15% of a child actor's earnings in a trust fund which no family member has access to. This law protects child actors from parents and family members who think they are entitled to take everything the child earns and have no plans for the future (when the child will be grown up and might not even be an actor anymore). Coogan continued to act and later secured one of his best known roles when he played Uncle Fester in the 1960s television series The Addams Family.

Silent film actress Olive Thomas had one of the most bizarre deaths in Hollywood history. She died as a consequence of unwittingly drinking her husband's syphilis medication.

The views of John Wayne on Native Americans were rather

blunt. "I don't feel we did wrong in taking this great country away from them, if that's what you're asking. Our so-called stealing of this country from them was just a matter of survival. There were great numbers of people who needed new land, and the Indians were selfishly trying to keep it for themselves. Look, I'm sure there have been inequalities. If those inequalities are presently affecting any of the Indians now alive, they have a right to a court hearing. But what happened 100 years ago in our country can't be blamed on us today."

Live ammunition was used in Old Hollywood movies. Bullets would be fired over the heads of actors when shooting action scenes.

Bing Crosby's son Gary Crosby (who was an actor himself and once appeared in The Twilight Zone) wrote a memoir in which he said his father was a cold and abusive man who would hit him with a metal studded belt until he drew blood. After Bing Crosby's death in 1977, Gary Crosby expressed no remorse and said his father was probably in Hell now. The wider Crosby family was rather split on Gary's claims of abuse. Bing Crosby's second wife and family were appalled by the claims and insisted that Bing Crosby was a kind and loving man. Gary was supported though by his siblings Lindsay and Dennis (both of whom later took their own lives). One of Gary's other brothers was not supportive though and believed that Gary's memoir was not an accurate portrayal of their father.

Some Like It Hot was banned in Kansas because of its cross-dressing theme.

Elizabeth Taylor was the first female actor to earn one million dollars for appearing in a film.

Veronica Lake was only 4'11 tall. Studio bios would pretend she was 5'3.

When they first started testing atomic bombs, the U.S military would paint Hollywood stars on them. Rita Hayworth was depicted on an early atomic bomb.

Joan Crawford, like most Hollywood stars, was paranoid about gaining weight. It was reported that as part of her diet her lunch consisted of few tablespoonfuls of cold consomme, a dish of rhubarb and half a dozen crackers.

The Soviet dictator Stalin was said to be a big fan of cowboy films.

Marlene Dietrich insured her vocal chords for more than $1 million.

It's a Wonderful Life might be the ultimate Christmas film but it was shot during the summer. The cast were sweltering.

Buddy Ebsen was originally cast as the Tin Man in The Wizard of Oz but the aluminum dust costume made him ill and he had to drop out and go to hospital.

Contracts were more constrictive in Old Hollywood. It was not uncommon for an actor to have a contract which bound them to a studio for several years.

Clark Gable disliked Gone With the Wind as he thought it was a 'film for women' and he was also fearful that his attempt to do a southern accent might be laughed at. He didn't have any great enthusiasm for the project and just did it for the money really.

Humphrey Bogart had to stand on a box shooting Casablanca because his co-star Ingrid Bergman was taller than him.

Silent comic Harold Lloyd lost two fingers when a prop bomb he was holding exploded.

The annual Academy Awards or Oscars were first held in 1929 at the Hollywood Roosevelt Hotel.

The singer and actor Mario Lanza was another Old Hollywood star who buckled under the studio pressure to stay thin. 'The look of Hollywood stars was important, and studios went to great lengths to keep their actors looking thin,' wrote Listverse. 'The most notorious example is Judy Garland, who, as an adolescent, was kept on an MGM-mandated diet of soup, coffee, and cigarettes, compensated by a steady supply of amphetamines to keep her energy levels up.Tenor-turned-actor Mario Lanza signed with MGM in the late 1940s and had a string of successful musicals that spawned million-selling hits. However, he also developed addictions to overeating and alcohol, which caused weight issues throughout his entire Hollywood career. Lanza would go on crash diets when it was time to film and put all the weight back on after shooting was done. This led to numerous health problems, which caused the singer to cancel multiple concerts and other live appearances.

During the late 1950s, Lanza moved to Rome to shoot several films and perform concerts throughout Europe. Like many times before, he had to lose weight, so he checked into a clinic. According to rumors, he underwent a dangerous procedure called twilight sleep in which he stayed under heavy sedation and was fed intravenously. Eventually, Lanza's body couldn't take it anymore. He died of a sudden heart attack in 1959. An unsubstantiated rumor quickly surfaced that he had been killed by the Mafia for reneging on a concert they were backing.'

That vaguely upper-crust transatlantic accent that a number of actresses in Old Hollywood had in movies was something that was encouraged by studios. Actresses would be given elocution and diction lessons to disguise their real voice.

Joan Crawford soaked her eyes in boric acid to give them more of a sparkle.

Painted cornflakes were used to depict snow in old movies.

Scotty Becket was one of the kids in the popular Our

Gang/Little Rascals series of shorts. He was acting from the age of four and signed a contract with MGM in the 1930s. His life rapidly went off the rails though - an all too familiar trope with child stars. He was arrested many times for drink driving, financial fraud, and was once caught trying to cross the Mexican border with illegal pills. He died at the age of 38 in 1968 after a suspected overdose.

Gene Kelly was said to be so rude to Debbie Reynolds on the set of Singing in the Rain that she used to go and cry under a piano between takes.

The musical producer Arthur Freed indecently exposed himself in his office to Shirley Temple when she moved to MGM. Temple was only eleven years-old at the time.

Stan Laurel was born in Lancashire and as a young man Stan joined Fred Karno's troop of music-hall performers where he learnt his trade and would sometimes understudy a certain Charlie Chaplin. Stan went back to Britain a few times before he made his career in the United States and actually appeared in early silent films with the Harlem, Georgia born Oliver Hardy - who was employed as a regular 'heavy' (villain) - without anyone seeing any potential in them forming a team. Although he is a brilliant performer and comedian, Stan looked set for a directing career until he was almost accidentally paired with Hardy and the seeds of a legendary partnership are sown. Despite his innocent and clueless onscreen persona, Stan was the brains of the organisation offscreen and would come up with many of the jokes and routines. He had a more difficult relationship with their legendary producer Hal Roach too and would battle him for creative control over their films and shorts.

The code regarding what was appropriate in movies came into force in 1934. Prior to this pre-code movies were allowed to depict sex, homosexuality, violence, drug use, or whatever they wanted.

In the mid 1930s, beautiful Frances Farmer was on course to become a major star. She married actor Leif Erickson and had been cast alongside Bing Crosby in a movie after plying her trade in B-pictures. However, Frances couldn't seem to stay out of trouble and deeper problems were on the horizon. She was fond of drinking and spent a night in jail for driving through a forbidden black out zone during the war. In the early 1940s she was arrested for dislocating the jaw of her hairdresser and in court she shoved a policeman and threw an inkwell at the judge. She was sent to the psychiatric ward at LA General Hospital and diagnosed with paranoid schizophrenia. She endured more hospitals and had electro-convulsive shock treatment. After her treatment she tried to stage a comeback a few times but her chance to become a superstar had long gone. She died of cancer in 1970.

When the Marx Brothers made their first film The Cocoanuts in 1929, sound equipment was so primitive that cameras were placed in sound proof booths to limit noise and so were limited in their freedom to move and follow the action. Maps and letters used in the film by characters are in reality soaked in water to prevent them from making any scrunching sounds!

Marilyn Monroe was one of the first celebrities who made it fashionable to lift weights as part of a daily exercise routine.

Shirley Temple was earmarked for the part of Dorothy in The Wizard of Oz but was annoyed to lose out to Judy Garland.

Alfred Hitchcock's horror film Pyscho was the very first to show a toilet on screen.

Clara Bow was one of the first superstars of early Hollywood. However, her life was difficult and dogged with salacious rumours. 'Clara Bow was known as the 'It Girl' and was the screen's first megastar international sex symbol,' said Reel Rundown. 'She was the first actress who visibly flaunted her sex appeal and, in turn, became the most talked-about resident of Hollywood. Idolized by Louise Brooks in the 20s,

Marilyn Monroe in the 50s, and Madonna in the 80s, Clara was an icon of sexual freedom for women everywhere. Her acting ability has been overshadowed by the scandalous stories which followed her. Most have been generally dismissed as urban legends, but Clara did give rumormongers grist for the mill. She scandalized image-conscious Hollywood peers by being successfully sued for alienation of affections by the wife of a doctor. In 1930, Bow herself sued a former secretary for embezzlement and, in retaliation, the secretary shocked the press with stories of Bow's USC goings on and, the same year, a newspaper ran a series of articles reporting how Bow frequently behaved inappropriately in her private life. She suffered her first nervous breakdown at age 26, and Paramount, the studio that had made a fortune on Bow, dropped the star in 1931.

The indifference of the studio added to Clara's difficult mental state already fragile from the publicity surrounding the scandals. This combined with the mental scars caused by her abusive family background (she had been raped by her father) and left Clara mentally unstable and incapacitated for the later years of her life. She died in solitude in 1965.'

The Fox studio dropped Shirley Temple when she was twelve years-old. They already thought she was a has-been!

Believe it or not, Adolf Hitler was said to be a big fan of Laurel & Hardy. It has also been claimed that Hitler was a fan of the Marx Brothers. This would be ironic as they were Jewish.

Audrey Hepburn trained to be a dental assistant before she became famous.

David O. Selznick was fined $5,000 for the line "Frankly my dear, I don't give a damn" in Gone with the Wind.

Use of amphetamines was rife in Old Hollywood because of the long hours that had to be worked.

Marilyn Monroe would have raw eggs for breakfast as part of her diet regime.

These days Hollywood stars often do their best to avoid the press but in Old Hollywood it was very different. As part of contracts in Old Hollywood, stars had to court the press and cater to their demands for photographs and quotes. In the old days the studios worked on the theory that all publicity was good publicity.

Kissing in Old Hollywood movies was something that was strictly controlled and never permitted to last very long. The code stipulated that kissing on screen could never display any sign of 'lust'.

La Dolce Vita star Anita Ekberg was a former fashion model and Miss Sweden and won a contract with Universal Studios after competing in the Miss Universe competition. She appeared in an Abbott and Costello film and a few other pictures but it was Fellini who made her world famous with La Dolce Vita, despite her assertion that "It was I who made Fellini famous, not the other way around!"

Jackie Cooper was a former child star whose career stretched from 1929 to 1987. You may know him as the Clark Kent's editor at the Daily Planet in the Christopher Reeve Superman films. In his memoir he said that when he was a child star a director once got him to cry in a scene by threatening to shoot his dog.

The late Dino De Laurentis (he of Flash Gordon, King Kong et al fame), who worked with Fellini at Cinecittà Studios as a young man, had suggested Paul Newman for the central role in La Dolce Vita but Fellini wasn't too impressed with that idea and preferred the far less well known Marcello Mastrioanni. Fellini felt that it would have been somewhat incongruous and strange to have Paul Newman as a nobody gossip columnist chasing after film stars.

Believe it or not, Cary Grant was later a great fan of the psychedelic drug LSD and said that it helped him a lot in his attempts to understand himself.

Marlene Dietrich was one of the first stars to be ordered to lose weight by the studio. She was put on a diet of broth, cottage cheese, and toast.

The 1956 sci-fi horror Invasion of the Body Snatchers is the ultimate fifties paranoia picture. What is most interesting about the film is that it is laced with a multitude of apparent hidden meanings on everything from the Communist Witchhunts to the FBI and yet the author of the original novel and the director always maintained that no grand political metaphor was intended and it was primarily just a science fiction story about aliens from outer space taking over human beings. A film about the loss of identity and how human beings are becoming more and more alike.

Margaret O'Brien's mother used an interesting tactic to make her daughter convincingly cry in the film Meet Me in St. Louis. "The way they got me to cry is that June Allyson and I were in competition as the best criers on the MGM lot. So when I was having trouble crying, my mother would come over to me and say, 'I'll have the makeup man put the false tears down your face, but June is such a great, great actress – she always cries real tears.' And then I started crying, because I couldn't let June win the competition."

Joan Collins said in her memoir that she was the prime candidate to play the title role in the 1963 film Cleopatra but was axed from the part because she refused to sleep with Buddy Adler, the head of 20th Century Fox. Collins, who had done more than one audition for the part, said she fled from the office of Adler in tears after he sexually propositioned her. Collins said that when she was a young actress she frequently had to fend off the lecherous and unwanted sexual advances of studio figures and actors.

Judy Garland was born Frances Ethel Gumm.

During World War 2, women working in American munitions factories were banned from adopting Veronica Lake's "peek-a-boo" hairdo because it was deemed dangerous (lest the hair should get caught in a machine).

According to legend, the dog in The Wizard of Oz actually got paid more money than the dwarves.

Shirley Temple made $3 million before she hit puberty.

Jean Harlow's diet was so strict that she would only eat raw tomatoes for lunch and dinner.

The scene in which Judy Garland sings "Over the Rainbow" in The Wizard of Oz almost ended up on the cutting room floor. it wasn't originally going to be in the film.

It was common for Hollywood studios to make up fictitious information about the background of the stars they had under contract. They were basically coming up with a product they could sell.

A pair of Los Angeles serial killers known as The Hillside Stranglers once let the daughter of the actor Peter Lorre go free because they calculated that murdering the relative of a celebrity would bring too much unwelcome attention to their activities.

Gloria Grahame was a big star at RKO. She was a rather eccentric actress who had what you might describe as a colourful and strange private life. 'Gloria Grahame is best known for her work at RKO in multiple noirs, and her supporting role in Frank Capra's It's a Wonderful Life, but her personal life was anything but,' wrote NewFairyBlog. 'Grahame's most scandalous exploit came when she married legendary director Nicholas Ray, and then had an affair with his thirteen year old son, Tony, which eventually led to their divorce in 1952. Grahame later married Tony, and her former step-son became the step-father of his half-brother. (I know). The couple stayed together for fourteen years (her longest marriage) before divorcing in 1974. During that marriage she became obsessed with plastic surgery, and at one point had to undergo electro-shock therapy after a nervous breakdown. She died in 1981 from breast cancer, after choosing not to seek treatment, at the age of 57.'

When Errol Flynn was in his late forties he had a girlfriend who was only fifteen years old.

Shirley Temple had to have 50 curls put into her hair each day when she was a child star.

Tippi Hedren says she was subject to sexual, mental and physical abuse from Alfred Hitchcock when she starred in the classic thriller film The Birds.

When the 1940s Marx Brothers comeback film A Night in Casablanca was announced, Warner Brothers tried to bully the movie into changing its name and threatened legal action. They felt that the title was too similar (and presumably too disrespectful) to their movie Casablanca. Groucho Marx wrote a letter to Warner Brothers in which he said it was ridiculous for the studio to try and claim ownership over a name. He also pointed out that the Marx Brothers were an act before Warner Brothers existed and suggested that maybe he should take legal action to stop Warners using the term 'Brothers' in their name!

In Old Hollywood, stars had to abide by penalty clauses in their contracts relating to weight gain and becoming pregnant.

Mary Astor is probably best known for The Maltese Falcon. She appeared in many films and was a great star of her era. In 1936 she became involved in a custody case and extracts from her diary became public. What was most shocking in the leaks was that Astor wrote about her steamy encounters with a man referred to as G or George. This was the married writer George S Kaufman. 'His first initial is G, and I fell like a ton of bricks,' she wrote in her diary. 'I met him Friday. Saturday he called for me at the Ambassador and we went to the Casino for lunch and had a very gay time! Monday—we ducked out of the boring party. It was very hot so we got a cab and drove around the park a few times and the park was, well, the park, and he held my hand and said he'd like to kiss me but didn't. Tuesday night we had a dinner at '21' and on the way to see Run Little Chillunhe did kiss me—and I don't think either of us remember much what the show was about. We played kneesies during the first two acts, my hand wasn't in my own lap during the third. It's been years since I've felt up a man in public, but I just got carried away.

Afterwards we had a drink someplace and then went to a little flat in 73rd Street where we could be alone, and it was all very thrilling and beautiful. Once George lays down his glasses, he is quite a different man. His powers of recuperation are amazing, and we made love all night long. It all worked perfectly, and we shared our fourth climax at dawn. I didn't see much of anybody else the rest of the time—we saw every show in town, had grand fun together and went frequently to 73rd Street where he f***** the living daylights out of me.'

Lucille Ball auditioned for the part of Scarlett O'Hara in Gone With the Wind.

Thomas Harper Ince was a silent film producer, director, screenwriter, and actor. Ince was known as the "Father of the Western" and was responsible for making over 800 films. He revolutionized the motion picture industry by creating the first major Hollywood studio facility and invented movie production by introducing the "assembly line" system of filmmaking. Ince's sudden death at 44, after he became severely ill aboard the private yacht of media tycoon William Randolph Hearst, has caused much speculation, although the official cause of his death was heart failure.

Actors in Old Hollywood did not have the freedom to decline parts in the same fashion that actors are today. Bette Davis, for example, was suspended by Warner Bros when she refused to do a film they'd arranged for her.

When she was at the height of her career as a child actor, there were genuine rumours that Shirley Temple was a highly talented dwarf actress who was merely pretending to be a child!

Ava Gardner, to the envy of other actors one would imagine, always had trouble putting on weight. Studio bigwigs wanted a few curves on their female stars so she was encouraged to gorge herself on chocolate, cheese, and whatever she wanted.

The distinctive looking actor Peter Lorre, best known for Casablanca, is alleged to have spent most of his career high on morphine. 'If you've ever seen a picture of Peter Lorre,' said Grunge, 'you've probably noticed his eyes: all droopy, like he's about to fall asleep. Lorre leveraged his weird looks into a long career playing oddballs and villains. But his distinctive expression may have had less to do with genetics and more to do with what the Casablanca actor was sticking in his arm. Lorre spent his entire career whacked out on morphine. His addiction started long before he ever graced a Hollywood screen, following an appendix operation in his native Europe.

According to the London Review of Books, his doctors kept the young actor so full of morphine that he wound up hopelessly addicted. By the time he appeared as the serial killer in Fritz Lang's disturbing German thriller M, Lorre's addiction was so well-known in acting circles that his friends joked the "M" stood for "morphine". He carried the addiction over with him when he transitioned to Hollywood, where he also got hooked on prescription pills and cough medicine. For stretches of his career, Lorre was even choosing roles based on how they interfered with his drug taking. He took the part of Mr. Moto in an eight-film series because he needed drug money, but also because they'd let him shoot up in his trailer. Whole films were shot with him so smacked out he could barely climb the stairs. And he still out-acted everybody else on set.'

Joan Crawford was born Lucille Fay LeSueur. It is said that she hated the name Joan Crawford (which the studio obviously chose for her).

Vertigo star Kim Novak said she was once at a party with Sammy Davis Jr. and Tony Curtis and woke up in the morning naked with no memory of what happened the night before. She believes that someone spiked her drink.

At the age of eight, Shirley Temple's mail averaged 16,000 letters a month and her birthday brought 167,000 presents from fans around the world.

Stage and silent actress Martha Mansfield was already a veteran with a long CV at the age of 24. Her career though was not destined to be a long one in chronological terms. In 1924 she died in a horrific accident while on the set of the film The Warrens of Virginia. Mansfield was sitting in a car wearing her elaborate period costume when a lit match set her dress ablaze. They pulled her from the car and extinguished the flames as quickly as possible but the burns were so severe she died the next morning. As ever in Hollywood the show must go on so studio executives simply ordered the film to continue shooting. Martha Mansfield had shot most of her scenes anyway before her bizarre death so there was no need to recast or reshoot.

Gloria Swanson was well ahead of her time when it came to health and nutrition. She was a vegetarian and a fan of yoga.

Starlets in Old Hollywood were giving acting and speaking classes as part of their preparation for movie stardom. It is often alleged that Clara Bow struggled when the silent film era ended because she had a thick Brooklyn accent.

Elizabeth Taylor was fond of a peanut butter and bacon

sandwich. This unusual food combination could be described as an acquired taste.

In one of his memoirs, the actor David Niven said that Errol Flynn liked to park his car outside of high schools so that he could sit and watch schoolgirls.

A 'morality' code on the depiction of sex in Old Hollywood meant there were a number of rules which had to be followed. Notice how in old films and TV shows a married couple sleep in separate beds? This is because productions were banned from showing two people in the same bed. Nudity, even in silhouette, was also banned.

Production on the film Hello Dolly! was a tense affair thanks to the mutual dislike between its stars Barbra Streisand and Walter Matthau. "I have more talent in my smallest fart than she does in her entire body," Matthau is alleged to have said.

Blonde, blue-eyed Gwili Andre from Denmark, "the highest priced model in America," was taken on as a "Garbo look-alike" by RKO Studio, earning $25,000 a year and dating Howard Hughes. To her dismay, she failed to become a movie star. In a bizarre suicide, she was found sprawled on the bedroom floor of her apartment, burned to a crisp in a funeral pyre she had made out of old publicity clippings. She was 51 years old. After years of desperately trying to resurrect her career Gwili Andre had given up and taken her life in a most theatrical way.

Bette Davis and Joan Crawford famously had a fierce rivalry and tense relationship. After the death of Crawford in 1977, Bette Davis said - "You should never say bad things about the dead, you should only say good. Joan Crawford is dead. Good."

Shirley Temple's studio sued the author Graham Greene when he wrote in a (rather astonishing and eccentric) review that Temple's film persona was deliberately sexual. "The owners of a child star are like leaseholders—their property diminishes in value every year," said Greene. "Time's chariot is at their back; before them acres of anonymity. Miss Shirley Temple's case, though, has a peculiar interest: infancy is her disguise, her appeal is more secret and more adult. Already two years ago she was a fancy little piece (real childhood, I think, went out after The Littlest Rebel). In Captain January she wore trousers with the mature suggestiveness of a Dietrich: her neat and well-developed rump twisted in the tap-dance: her eyes had a sidelong searching coquetry. Now in Wee Willie Winkie, wearing short kilts, she is completely totsy. Watch her swaggering stride across the Indian barrack-square: hear the gasp of excited expectation from her antique audience when the sergeant's palm is raised: watch the way she measures a man with agile studio eyes, with dimpled depravity. Adult emotions of love and grief glissade across the mask of childhood, a childhood that is only skin-deep. It is clever, but it cannot last. Her admirers—middle-aged men and clergymen —respond to her dubious coquetry, to the sight of her well-shaped and desirable little body, packed with enormous vitality, only because the safety curtain of story and dialogue drops between their intelligence and their desire."

Lupe Vélez got her start in the late silent era and went on to star in RKO's popular Mexican Spitfire series. Sadly, she's most famous for Kenneth Anger claiming in Hollywood Babylon that she drowned when her head got stuck in her toilet. This was of course absolute nonsense like much of Hollywood Babylon. Biographer Michelle Vogel debunked this urban myth in her book on the actress. 'The truth?' Vogel writes. 'Lupe Velez died in her bed, as she intended. She was 36 years-old, unmarried and about to become a mother. She was successful, beautiful, kind, talented, funny, a little bit crazy (by her own admission), and on December 14, 1944, she was dead by her own hand. Every ounce of the truth was tragic. No salacious embellishment needed.'

In his 'tell all' book Full Service: My Adventures in Hollywood and the Secret Sex Lives of the Stars, Scotty Bowers claims that he had a very passionate encounter with Vivien Leigh.

"We screwed as though the survival of the world depended on it. Vivien could not control herself. She was loud. She would squeal and holler and laugh. She had [spasm] after [spasm], and each one was noisier than the last. She yelled and called out louder and louder... this was one of the best f**** I had ever had."

Alma Rubens (1897–1931) was a film actress and stage performer. Rubens was a huge star in the twenties but her career was ruined by drugs. She died of lobar pneumonia and bronchitis shortly after being arrested for cocaine possession in January 1931. Rubens even wrote a memoir with the (unforgettable) title - Why I Remain a Dope Fiend: The Most Amazing Confession Ever Told!

Charlie Chaplin's fondness for much younger women would raise a lot of eyebrows if he was around today. 'Sexually abusing and exploiting young women is nothing new in Hollywood scandals, and the biggest star of the silent era proves that,' wrote AllThatsInteresting. 'Comedy genius Charlie Chaplin became a worldwide icon early on in his life and this, in turn, messed with his head, at least when it came to women. He boasted of his conquests relentlessly and claimed, shamelessly, that he had slept with more than 2,000 women over the course of his life. He wasn't out looking for love either. When asked in an interview to describe his ideal women, Chaplin replied – "I am not exactly in love with her, but she is entirely in love with me." Mature women might have been harder for Chaplin to charm, but they were not his target. Chaplin was after young girls. His first high profile romance involved his 19-year-old co-star Edna Purviance. Four years later, when he was 29, Chaplin met the 16-year-old child actress Mildred Harris and promptly forgot all about Edna.

Shirley Temple said that when she became a teenager and got rid of her curls, Hollywood bigwigs were horrified at how plain she suddenly looked. They even made her pin her ears back. She quit acting in her twenties and later became a diplomat.

In his autobiography Life is Too Short, veteran star Mickey Rooney was maybe a little too candid when discussing his former flames. This led to some fairly bizarre and eccentric passages. "We were both athletic in bed, and pretty verbal, too. Once Ava (Gardner) lost her Southern reticence, she seemed to enjoy using the f-word. And I didn't mind a bit, when, for example, she would look me straight in the eye, raise a provocative eyebrow, and say, "Let's ****, Mickey. Now." Some years later, Hedda Hopper would say of Ava, "That girl was made to love and be loved." I had to agree with that judgement. Oh, we told ourselves that we were very much in love, and our sex life helped us in that particular piece of self-deception. Once Ava got into the spirit of things, she wanted to do it all the time. And she quickly learned what it was that turned me on about her.

Let me count the ways: a smouldering look, a laugh, a tear, kicking off her shoes as soon as she got in the house, getting all dolled up, not getting all dolled up, coming down to breakfast in a pair of shorts—and no top at all. In bed, let's just say that Ava was...well, she had this little rosebud down there at the center of her femininity that seemed to have a life of its own. I am not talking about muscles. One gal I knew had trained her muscles, so that she could snap carrots in her *****, not hands. But Ava had something different. She had this little extra—it was almost like a little warm mouth—that would reach up and grab me and take me in and make my, uh, my heart swell. She also had big brown nipples, which, when she was aroused, stood out like some double-long golden California raisins. And I sucked those warm breasts, I did taste her mother's milk."

About a week before his death in a car crash, James Dean had lunch with the actor Alec Guinness. Dean showed Alec Guiness his Porsche and Guiness had a dreadful premonition that Dean would be killed in that car. He told James Dean not to drive the car. Dean obviously this ignored this advice though. If he'd listened to Alec Guinness the fatal crash never would have happened.

Silent film star Nita Naldi followed an eccentric diet in which she would only eat lamb and pineapple.

The young JD Salinger (the famously reclusive author of The Catcher in the Rye) wanted to marry the 17-year-old Oona O'Neill (who was a noted beauty at the time and being tested by film studios) but while Salinger was away during the war she married a 53-year-old Charlie Chaplin instead. Salinger was absolutely furious and loathed Chaplin for it. A letter he wrote at the time (which only came to light in 1987) expressed Salinger's bitterness at the whole affair. 'I can see them at home evenings. Chaplin squatting grey and nude, atop his chiffonier, swinging his thyroid around his head by his bamboo cane, like a dead rat. Oona in an aquamarine gown, applauding madly from the bathroom.' Holden Caulfield's distaste for Hollywood and actors is said to come directly from Salinger losing O'Neill (later to become Lady Chaplin) to silver haired megastar and rascal Chaplin.

Believe it or not, the snow you see in The Wizard of Oz is actually pure asbestos. It was common in Old Hollywood to use asbestos.

THE SECRETS OF HARRY POTTER

When the film version of Harry Potter and the Philosopher's Stone was being planned, Steven Spielberg looked set to direct at one point. Spielberg spent around six months developing the film but his idea to make it as an animated feature was not what the studio or JK Rowling wanted. He eventually left the project. "I just felt that I wasn't ready to make an all-kids movie and my kids thought I was crazy," said Spielberg. "And the books were by that time popular, so when I dropped out, I knew it was going to be a phenomenon. But, you know I don't make movies because they're gonna to be phenomenons. I make movies because they have to touch me in a way that really commits me to a year, two years, three years of work."

Alan Horn, the president of Warner Bros when the Potter films were first optioned, said that no one there liked Steven Spielberg's idea of mashing up a couple of books into one story and doing it as an animated film. Harry Potter producer David Heyman says that, when he was attached to the first film as director, Steven Spielberg wanted to cast Haley Joel Osment (then a successful American child actor) as Harry Potter. David Heyman said he had a meeting with Spielberg about Harry Potter but never got the impression that Spielberg was very enthusiastic about the project or seemed especially keen or determined to actually do it. It came as no great surprise to Heyman when Spielberg decided to go and do something else instead.

Steven Spielberg said that one of the reasons why he decided not to make the first Harry Potter film was that he didn't consider it to be a big enough challenge. "I purposely didn't do the Harry Potter movie because for me, that was shooting ducks in a barrel. It's just a slam dunk. It's just like withdrawing a billion dollars and putting it into your personal bank accounts. There's no challenge." Spielberg has expressed no regrets about turning the film down in the end.

Disney bid for the Harry Potter film rights but did not get them because JK Rowling felt they wanted too much creative control. She wanted to retain some creative input into any films made from the books. Disney must have greatly regretted this later because they couldn't use Harry Potter in their theme parks. One of the stipulations that JK Rowling made when she sold the film rights was that any films had to be based on the stories in the books. She didn't want some studio to get the rights to the Harry Potter characters and then just make up their own stories and scripts.

Terry Gilliam (of Time Bandits and Monty Python fame) was JK Rowling's choice to direct the first Harry Potter film. Gilliam was on a shortlist of potential directors but the studio did not want him. "I was the perfect person to do Harry Potter," Gilliam complained. "I remember leaving the meeting, getting in my car, and driving for about two hours along Mulholland Drive just so angry. I mean, Chris Columbus' versions are terrible. Just dull. Pedestrian."

Terry Gilliam said that he was irritated by the fact the studio met with him despite having no intention of hiring him. He felt they just wanted to cross him from their list and be able to say they spoke to him. Gilliam is a famously forthright and independent sort of character who has been known to go over budget, bicker with studios, and spent too long on something. Gilliam was not the sort of person that could be micro-managed (whether you liked the end result or not, you would have got Gilliam's own vision for Harry Potter - not some diluted studio product) and this scared the studio away. They simply wanted a more conservative and mainstream choice that they would be able to control more.

American child actor Liam Aiken was the initial choice of the director Chris Columbus to play Harry Potter in the first film. Columbus had worked with Aitken before. However, JK

Rowling insisted that the parts had to be played by British actors so that all the accents would be authentic. A tentative offer to Aitken was withdrawn. Aitken was the only American who was in contention to play Harry. Rowling's insistence on British actors meant some big Hollywood stars had their hopes of being in the film dashed. Robin Williams was very keen to play Hagrid but JK Rowling already had her heart set on Robbie Coltrane for this part.

Tim Roth passed on the role of Professor Severus Snape to play General Thade in Tim Burton's Planet of the Apes. With the gift of hindsight, that seems like a very bad decision. Tim Burton's Planet of the Apes turned out to be a very forgettable film. Casting director Janet Hirshenson says there was a big push by the studio to cast Billy Elliot star Jamie Bell as Harry in the first film. However, at 14, Bell was ultimately considered a bit on the old side to play the young Harry at the start of his wizarding adventures.

Zoe Wanamaker, who played games mistress Madam Hooch in the first Potter film, did not return in the sequels because her character was written out of the franchise after Wanamaker was openly critical of what she perceived to be low rates of pay for the actors. It is said that, for Harry Potter and Chamber of Secrets, Daniel Radcliffe was to be only paid £125,000 until the actors' union Equity negotiated a better deal. Radcliffe ended up being paid two million pounds for the film.

Ian Hart, who played Professor Quirrell, also seemed to suggest that he wasn't paid much money to be in Harry Potter. "Warner Bros – I'm not going to slag them off – it was a long time ago now, but what Zoe Wanamaker said about the pay, knowing that they were going to make a fortune, they were still paying you as if you were just a trivial English actor, and for brokering that notion on television and in the press, I don't think she was invited back for the other films. What I'm trying to say is, that everyone was cosy and loads of people made a ton of money, but I didn't. Even in the first film, I had no leverage, because I wasn't in the next fourteen films, so I had no leverage. I knew I was dead. They paid me and let me go. That was fine, I enjoyed it. I had a good time and I enjoyed it, so I have no complaints."

When the first Harry Potter film was due for release, Warner Brothers began to take action against fan websites which used the name Harry Potter so that they could have exclusive control over this domain name. Their actions were criticised for being heavy-handed and mean-spirited, especially as the people who set up these websites were the fans who helped made Harry Potter the phenomenon it was. The Black Sisters in Harry Potter were probably inspired by the real life Mitford Sisters Unity and Diana. The Mitfords were from an aristocratic English family of socialites and became notorious for their support of fascism. Unity Mitford worshipped Adolf Hitler while Diana Mitford married British fascist leader Oswald Mosley.

There are some unmistakable similarities between Harry Potter and The Worst Witch by Jill Murphy. The Worst Witch was a series of books first published in the early 1970s. In the 1980s there was a TV film and in the 1990s a TV series based on the books. io9.com wrote the following: 'In this precursor to the Potter books, a young girl from a Mugg – uh – non-magical family attends a boarding school for witches. Which is in an ancient castle surrounded by an enchanted forest. While Mildred Hubble is enrolled at Miss Cackle's Academy for Witches, where she attends Potions, Broomstick Flying, Chants and Charms classes, she must deal with conflicts with her classmates, a cursed broom, and an attempt to overthrow the school. Also, Mildred and her friends make an invisibility potion. Similarities, include the fact that there's a mean teacher who hates the main character, and a popular blond kid who gets off on the wrong foot with the hero on the very first day. Is there a Case? The series of Worst Witch books skews younger and tends to the lighter side of magic than the Harry Potter books. Many of the similarities are of the superficial, non-copyrightable type, though Murphy got there first.'

When the first film came out in Britain, Peter Smith, general secretary of the Association of Teachers and Lecturers, managed to get himself in the news by warning about the themes of Harry Potter. "Increasing numbers of children are spending hours alone browsing the Internet in search of satanic websites. ATL is concerned that nobody is monitoring this growing fascination. The surge in interest in the occult is, at its best, a welcome stimulus to children's imagination and personal growth. Children, particularly girls on the cusp of puberty, have always been interested in magic and in parallel worlds.

"Casting spells gives them a feeling of control over an increasingly confusing world at a time when many youngsters feel powerless. But there is a darker side to the occult which may disturb vulnerable children and expose them to manipulation by adults. Parents and teachers will want to educate young people about the dangers of dabbling in the occult, before they become too deeply involved. The Harry Potter movie will lead to a whole new generation of youngsters discovering witchcraft and wizardry. We welcome the values this will ingrain, focusing on good triumphing over evil. Though it is important not to over-react to this fun and entertaining phenomenon, the risks are clear. Children must be protected from the more extreme influences of the occult and be taught in a responsible and positive way the risks of journeying into the unknown."

An outbreak of lice occurred among the child cast members during the filming of Harry Potter and the Chamber of Secrets. Ian McKellen says he was approached to play Dumbledore when Richard Harris passed away. Nothing came of this though and Michael Gambon got the part in the end. McKellen had already played a famous wizard with his role as Gandalf in the Lord of the Rings films. Ian McKellen later said he would never have played Dumbledore because Richard Harris was critical of him and he wouldn't want to step into the shoes of an actor who had disdain for him.

Emma Watson says she felt guilty growing up for not enjoying fame very much. She felt it was all wasted on her. Rupert Grint says he enjoyed the Harry Potter experience more on the early films than the later ones. "For the first few Harry Potter films I was living the dream. The reason I auditioned was because I loved the books. When I got to film three or four, I started to feel an overwhelming weight of responsibility because they were so phenomenally popular. The whole press and red carpet thing was an attack on the senses. I don't excel in that kind of environment."

Warner Brothers had to re-sign their main cast again on Harry Potter And The Order Of The Phoenix because the principal actors were only signed for four films at the start of the franchise. When Emma Watson's contract came up for renewal in 2006 they persuaded her to stay by altering her schedule so that she could sit her school exams. "It was mainly to do with scheduling and I had a real fight on my hands to ensure that I was able to go to university and I was able to sit my A-levels, because the schedule they handed to me didn't really allow for any of that and I just wasn't prepared to let it go. They essentially moved the Harry Potter film schedule around my exam dates, which was amazing. It all worked out."

Jamie Waylett played Vincent Crabbe in six of the Harry Potter films but did not return for the last movies in the franchise. This is because Waylett was arrested for possession of drugs in 2009. He was also convicted for participating in riots that occurred in south London around this time. Waylett received a two year prison sentence. The Harry Potter movies remain Waylett's only credits and it appears as if his acting career is finished.

Rob Knox was a young English actor who was born in Kent in 1989. His first credited role was in the ITV police show The Bill and he also had an uncredited part in the 2004 Clive Owen film King Arthur. He had a huge break in 2008 when he was cast as Marcus Belby in the movie Harry Potter and the Half-Blood Prince. Knox had also signed to appear in the next movie - Harry Potter and the Deathly Hallows (which was eventually split into two parts). Knox must have been pretty excited at the thought of the career options and money that might come his way out of the Harry Potter association. Fate was to intervene in heartless fashion though.

On 24 May 2008, Rob Knox was in his home town of Sidcup and during a night out intervened to protect his brother from a man who was threatening him with two knives. The man was twenty-two year-old Karl Bishop. A few weeks earlier, Bishop had apparently had an altercation with Knox and accused him of stealing a phone (which he hadn't). Karl Bishop was basically a lunatic with no moral compass. He was a wild and feral character and a sociopath. Sociopaths lack a sense of responsibility or a social conscience. They are prone to antisocial behaviour. They can then tilt into becoming a psychopath. A psychopath has even less of a moral compass than a sociopath. Sociopaths do not have a rational and logical voice in their head telling them that a course of action is wrong. They will ignore and banish any such thoughts. They have no empathy, thought, or remorse for their victims.

The tragic night in question, Knox had rugby tackled Bishop to protect his brother Jamie. Bishop then stabbed Knox in the buttock and four times in the chest. The fatal blow apparently came when Bishop - who was clearly completely crazy - stabbed Knox in the head. Others who tried to intervene were also stabbed by Bishop - one receiving spinal injuries and another knife wounds to the face. The friends of Rob Knox were very brave that night because, at great risk to themselves, they eventually managed to restrain Bishop long enough for the police to arrive. Sadly though, the injuries to Rob Knox were so severe he died. Knox was just eighteen years-old.

Karl Bishop was sentenced to life for the murder of Rob Knox. He showed no remorse in court and smirked and smiled during the trial. He was a truly vile and despicable person with no compassion or humanity at all. Bishop was one of those people where you really hope he never gets out of prison. It transpired that Bishop always carried knives and had been wanted in connection with a robbery he conducted at knifepoint. It wasn't much consolation to the family of Rob Knox but at least this dangerous and awful young man was behind bars and no longer a danger to society.

The heartbroken family of Rob Knox said that it was typical of his character that he had sacrificed his life trying to protect others. His death prompted the British government to announce new measures cracking down on knife crimes and the possession of these dangerous weapons. Sadly though, knife crime is a problem that seems to never go away. Why anyone would go out carrying knives (let alone use them to hurt people) is a baffling mystery to most normal people but - alas - it still seems to happen.

Rupert Grint says he considered leaving the Potter film franchise a couple of times. "There were definitely times when I thought about leaving. Filming Harry Potter was a massive sacrifice; working from such a young age for such long periods and I definitcly remember thinking during one extended break, 'This whole thing is so all consuming, do I really want to go back? Maybe it's just not for me.' I guess I was probably just being a teenager."

Rupert Grint said he felt a bit lost for a time when the film series ended. He didn't quite know what to do with himself. Grint says it was hard to adjust to life after Harry Potter. "The line between Ron and me became thinner with each film and I think we became virtually the same person. There's a lot of me in Ron and moving on was a massive adjustment because it was such a constant part of my life. I don't want to liken it to coming out of prison because it wasn't a prison, but it did feel like stepping out of an institution. It was nice to breathe the fresh air and now I'm really enjoying stepping further away from that blue-screen world."

After his death, Alan Rickman's diaries were eventually arranged to be published. His comments about the Potter franchise were often very frank. Rickman didn't seem to think Daniel Radcliffe was much of an actor, was critical of Emma Watson's diction, and seemed to think the Harry Potter director David Yates was a hack. Rickman seemed to think the first film in the franchise was atrocious and called John Williams' score 'hideous'. Rickman said in his diaries that he had tried to get out of his Harry Potter contract a couple of times but they always kept insisting that he had to come back.

MURDER

On January 15, 1947, a body was discovered on a street in Los Angeles. The body was that of a young dark haired woman. She had been sliced in half, had her blood removed, and her mouth cut into a Joker smile. A tattoo had been cut from her thigh and stuffed in her private parts. It was a grisly and shocking murder worthy of Jack the Ripper. The police managed to identify the victim through fingerprints. Her name was Elizabeth Short - though in the wake of this case she would become immortal as the Black Dahlia. The Black Dahlia mystery baffled the police. Not only was the murder brutal and gruesome it also indicated a degree of medical knowledge (the relative proximity of a medical school close to where the body was found led the police to suspect the killer might have a connection to this establishment).

The killer was deemed to be cunning, intelligent, and most likely completely insane. Elizabeth had been missing for six days when her body was found. It is presumed then that the killer kidnapped and then tortured her before the murder. The police found out that Elizabeth Short was working as a waitress at the time of her death. Like so many people she had moved to Los Angeles to become a star but she found that acting jobs were hard to come by and so she ended up waiting tables to make ends meet.

About a week after the grisly discovery of the body, a letter was sent to the local newspaper containing some of Elizabeth Short's personal belongings. The contents had been cleaned with petrol - which was also how the killer had cleaned Short's body before he dissected it. It was pretty obvious then that the sender of this letter was the killer. How else would they have Elizabeth Short's personal affects? The police, thanks partly to these personal affects, manage to obtain the details of dozens of men that Elizabeth Short had known but investigations into these men turned out to be a frustrating dead end. The case eventually went cold. The killer was never caught. There are theories though. One theory contends that Short's murder was connected to The Cleveland Torso Murderer.

The Cleveland Torso Murderer is one of the grisliest serial killers never captured. Some suspect that this killer might have murdered Elizabeth Short. The killer was active from 1935 to 1938 and killed between twelve and twenty victims. This killer killed both men and women. The targets were chosen very carefully in that they were drifters or homeless people so wouldn't be missed. The victims were dismembered and beheaded. The male victims were castrated. Some of the victims had a chemical agent applied to them.

The Cleveland Torso Murderer is credited with twelve official murders but may have killed twenty people in all. There is a theory that this may have been the work of more than one killer but the truth was never really established. The famous lawman Eliot Ness was in charge of the investigation to catch the killer. At one point the killer even left the remains of one victim outside of the office building where Ness worked - simply to taunt Ness. Because the bodies were often found some time after death and many of the heads had been removed this made identification of the victims almost impossible at times. In fact, only a couple of victims were ever identified.

The main suspect in the case was Dr Francis Sweeney. It is said that Ness thought Sweeney was the killer. Sweeney was a former medic in the army who had performed amputations in combat zones. Sweeney also failed a lie detector test when he was in police custody. However, Sweeney was never charged or prosecuted for the murders - apparently because Ness thought there was little chance of securing a conviction. One thing that complicated matters was that Dr Sweeney was a cousin of Congressman Martin L. Sweeney. Congressman Martin L. Sweeney was known for his dislike of Eliot Ness and wouldn't have taken too kindly to these murders being pinned on a relative.

Dr Sweeney was therefore not put on trial. He was bitter at his treatment by Ness and sent Ness threatening letters until he died. A man named Frank Dolezal was actually arrested for the murders and had a confession beaten out of him but it transpired that he was innocent. Dolezal is believed to attracted suspicion because he knew one of the victims. The question of who The Cleveland Torso Murderer really was therefore remains a mystery. All we really do know is that this was an especially disturbed and grisly killer who clearly enjoyed the attention his crimes were affording him. He was one of the deadliest serial killers never to be captured.

The same year that Elizabeth Short was murdered, a woman named Jeanne French was found dead in Los Angeles. She had been stomped to death and a cryptic message was scrawled on her body in lipstick. Some believe that the deaths of Short and French are connected and that they both encountered the same killer. The police did not believe in this theory themselves though and felt these two deaths were not connected but simply disconnected tragedies. Naturally, the police had to deal with a lot of time wasters during their investigation into Short's murder. Many people came forward to claim they had killed Elizabeth Short but were then revealed to be fantasists or liars. There are a number of genuine suspects in the Elizabeth Short murder case but the actual killer has never been verified.

Among the Black Dahlia suspects are Walter Bayley. Bayley was a surgeon who lived only a few minutes away from where Short's body was found. He was suffering from a degenerative brain disease at the time. This has led to a theory that he was acting in a crazy unhinged manner. The counter argument is that the 67 year-old Bayley was not really in any fit state to carry out a murder like this - which would have required planning, stealth, and physical strength. Bayley's status as a Black Dahlia suspect comes from the fact that he had medical training (so would have known how to dissect a body) and also easy access to properties in the area where Short was disposed of.

Another suspect was a bellhop and former mortician's assistant named Leslie Dillon. Dillon began writing to Los Angeles Police Department psychiatrist Dr. J. Paul De River with his theories about Short's murder. Dillon's detailed knowledge of the case and obvious dark fascination with sex and sadism led the police to believe he could well be a suspect. Dillon even claimed he knew the man that had killed Elizabeth Short. Dr. J. Paul De River took this claim to be a proxy confession by Dillon. Dillon was placed in custody at one point and many detectives came to suspect he was the killer. The stumbling block though was that Dillon's whereabouts at the time of the murder could not be proven. It could not be established that he was in Los Angeles and so there was no case against him without this evidence.

Another suspect in Short's death was Mark Hansen. Hansen was a nightclub owner and Elizabeth Short's landlord. It transpired that he was one of the last people she spoke to before she went missing. The police believed that Hansen was infatuated with Short but she'd rebuffed his romantic and sexual advances. What made the police especially interested in Hansen was that he was friends with a number of doctors and there was evidence that as a young man he had attended a medical school. One can see how these details, when factored in with his personal connection to Elizabeth Short, made Hansen a person of interest. Mark Hansen died in 1964. He was never charged with Short's murder. The police detectives from the time and in recent years who have studied the case seem to have conflicting views concerning Hansen as a suspect. Some believe he murdered Short and others think he was a red herring who had nothing to do with the case.

Dr. Patrick O'Reilly was an interesting suspect in the Black Dahlia murder case. O'Reilly was a doctor who was friends with Mark Hansen. They apparently visited sex parties together. It seems reasonable to presume then that O'Reilly must have known Elizabeth Short. O'Reilly had criminal charges for violent sexually motivated crimes and he certainly had the medical knowledge required to dissect and clean a dead body. Despite all of these apparent connective details though he was never charged with having anything to do with Short's murder. O'Reilly was married to the daughter of a police captain. This has led to theories of a police cover-up.

George Hodel was also a suspect and placed under police surveillance at one point. Hodel was a physician accused of raping his teenage daughter. He was known to be a dodgy and troubled sort of character. The police manage to get some evidence that Elizabeth Short may have been one of George Hodel's patients. In the end though the evidence collected was not sufficient for a formal charge or a trial. Steve Hodel, George HJodel's son, later wrote a book in which he claimed his father was the killer of Elizabeth Short. Steve Hodel then rather damaged what little credibility he had by writing another book in which he claimed his father was also the Zodiac killer. These books were taken with what you might describe as a pinch of salt. I daresay Hodel is now working on a book claiming his father had access to a time machine and was Jack the Ripper.

George Knowlton is often listed as a Black Dahlia murder suspect - thanks mainly to the efforts of his daughter. Janice Knowlton claimed that her father George murdered and dissected Elizabeth Short in their garage. Janice Knowlton (inevitably) wrote a book about this and said that Elizabeth Short was a sex worker who would find children for child abuse gangs. Janice Knowlton claimed that she was later sold to a sex gang herself and ended up being abused by no lesser figure than Walt Disney. Janice Knowlton died in a prescription drugs overdose in 2004. The police were never terribly convinced by her claims concerning her father although they did arrange a dig at her childhood home. Nothing suspicious relating to a murder was found on the property though.

Other theories include the possibility that Elizabeth Short was killed by a woman that she may have been sharing a room with and fallen out with. This theory doesn't explain though why this disgruntled room mate would have then undertook such a grisly and complicated - not to mention risky - manner of disposing of the body. Donald H. Wolfe wrote in his 2006 book The Mob, the Mogul, and the Murder That Transfixed Los Angeles, that Elizabeth Short was murdered by the gangster Bugsy Siegel, at the request of newspaper publisher Norman Chandler. Short, so the theory goes, was pregnant with Chandler's child and so Chandler wanted to get rid of her.

There is no evidence though which connects Bugsy Siegel to the murder of Elizabeth Short. The craziest theory concerning this murder was that proposed by a childhood friend of Elizabeth Short. He concluded that the killer in this awful case was none other than the film director Orson Welles! The real truth about the Black Dahlia case has yet to be verified. It's a case which seems set to keep armchair detectives busy for many years to come.

Bob Crane was the star of sixties sitcom Hogan's Heroes. The show was about Allied prisoners of war in Germany who are always up to various schemes and trying to help the war effort for the Allies. The show ended in 1971 and Crane's career hit the doldrums soon after. He had a new TV show but that was axed after only thirteen episodes. Crane appeared in a Disney movie in the 1970s called Superdad but his son believes that Crane's private life nixed any chances of regular work for Disney. "He was doing a very bad Disney movie called Superdad, playing an all-American character who cares about his daughter running off with some unsavory type, but at Disney studios, in Burbank, he's on the set showing photographs of women that he's been with to people on the crew. That hurt him because the executives found out. People talk, and it started getting in publications like the National Enquirer."

In 1978, Bob Crane was found dead in a motel room in Scottsdale, Arizona. He was 49 years-old. Crane had been beaten to death with a camera tripod and had an electrical cord tied around his neck. Around fifty videotapes were also found of Crane having sex with various women. The biggest suspect in the case was a man named John Carpenter (not the famous director, this was another John Carpenter). Carpenter supplied Crane with video equipment and was also a fan of making amateur porn films. The night that Bob Crane died, Carpenter had been seen with Crane in a bar. However, Carpenter was found not guilty at a trial and DNA evidence tested decades later seemed to confirm his innocence. The bizarre death of Bob Crane therefore, for now, remains a mystery.

Rebecca Schaeffer was a 21 year-old actress in 1989 and starring in the CBS sitcom My Sister Sam. Schaeffer was up for a part in The Godfather III and had appeared in Woody Allen's Radio Days. She seemed destined to use her sitcom fame as a springboard to a movie carer. Schaeffer resided in the Fairfax District of Los Angeles and had an apartment in a Mock Tudor house. One day, Schaeffer heard her doorbell and rushed down thinking it was a script she was expecting to be delivered that day. Instead she found a young man outside the house who turned out to be a fan who had tracked her down. She signed an autograph for him and then he left.

Later in the afternoon, the young man returned and rang Schaeffer's bell again. This time, Rebecca Schaeffer was more short with him. She told the young man that he was wasting her precious time with these interruptions and that he should leave her alone. At this, the young man produced a gun and shot Schaeffer in the chest. She was taken to hospital but dead within an hour. The young-man who had killed Rebecca Schaeffer was 19 year-old Robert John Bardo. Bardo had become obsessed with Rebecca Schaeffer and once even tried to get onto the set of My Sister Sam. Bardo's motivation for the murder was his anger that Schaeffer had done a love scene in the film Scenes from the Class Struggle in Beverly Hills

Bardo went back to his home in Tuscon after the murder but was swiftly arrested by the police. One of Bardo's sisters knew that her brother suffered from mental illness and was obsessed with Rebecca Schaeffer. When she heard that Schaeffer had been murdered she immediately suspected her brother and called the police. Bardo was found guilty of first degree murder and sentenced to life imprisonment without the possibility of parole. The most chilling thing about this awful case was the ease with which Bardo managed to find out where Schaeffer lived.

Bardo had hired a private investigator and the investigator simply found Schaeffer's address through the California Department of Motor Vehicles. The tragic death of Rebecca Schaeffer triggered new anti-stalking laws. As a result of Rebecca's murder, Congress passed the Driver's Privacy Protection Act (which prohibits state Departments of Motor Vehicles from revealing the home addresses of state residents). The damage had already been done though. The murder of Rebecca Schaeffer remains one of the most chilling examples of 'stalking' ever recorded in Hollywood.

Dominique Dunne portrayed Dana Freeling in the 1982 horror film Poltergeist. She had also been cast as Robin Maxwell in the television miniseries V (this popular miniseries was about seemingly humanoid and friendly aliens who come to Earth and turn out to be blood-drinking lizards who want to take over). Dunne was the sister of the actor Griffin Dunne. Her father was the famous journalist Dominick Dunne. Around the time that V was in pre-production and about to start shooting in 1982, Dominique Dunne was 22 and in a relationship with a chef named John Sweeney. This relationship had become quite intense and Dominique Dunne decided she wanted to end it.

Sweeney met Dominique Dunne in a residence they used to share and begged for her to give him another chance. She refused to do this and insisted that their relationship was over for good. Sweeney was so enraged by this that he throttled the actress for what was later determined to be at least four minutes in the driveway of the house. Dominique Dunne passed out and was put in a coma. She died in hospital for days later. To the amazement of the family of Dominique

Dunne, John Sweeney was convicted of voluntary manslaughter and only served three years in prison. It felt like a ludicrously light punishment for what appeared to be a case of murder. John Sweeney changed his name and tried to resume his career as a chef after his release. Dominique Dunne's family though hired private detectives to keep track of Sweeney and let any new employers or friends he found know who he really was. It would not bring back Dominique, but at the very least they were extracting some sort of revenge on Sweeney.

Adrienne Shelly was an actress and director probably best known for her performances in Hal Hartley's The Unbelievable Truth (1989) and Trust (1990) and also the film Waitress. Although she was not a huge star she was one of those people that you'd recognise if you saw a picture of her. Adrienne Shelly was a 5'1 strawberry blonde and had a likeable and appealing screen presence. Shelly was highly acclaimed for her work in the film industry and very talented. It seems certain that she would have gone on to become much more famous and give many more great performances in movies. She also appeared in television shows like Homicide: Life on the Street and Oz.

On November 1, 2006 Adrienne Shelly was found dead in the shower of her New York apartment. She was 40 years old. Adrienne Shelly was found hanged in the shower and the police ruled it was a suicide. This verdict was strongly disputed though by her husband Andy Ostroy. He insisted that his wife was perfectly happy and had no reason to take her own life. Ostroy also said that Adrienne Shelly would never have killed herself and left their young two-year old daughter without a mother. The day before her death, Adrienne Shelly had thrown a Halloween party and seemed happy and cheerful. Her career was going great too so why on earth would she suddenly kill herself? It didn't make any sense.

Upon further investigation the police found a sneaker footprint in the bathroom which indicated another person had been present there. The husband of Adrienne Shelly turned out to be right. There was indeed foul play. This case required much more investigating. The sneaker footprint belonged to Diego Pillco, a 19-year-old construction worker from Ecuador. The precise details of what happened were never really established because Pillco changed his story several times while in custody but the general theory seems to be that he was interrupted by Adrienne Shelly while robbing her apartment and then felt he had to silence her to stop her from screaming or alerting the police.

Pillco tried to make it look as if she had committed suicide by hanging her body in the shower. Thankfully, his ruse was uncovered in the end and justice was served. The method of murder was believed to be strangulation - which made the early mistaken verdict of suicide even more puzzling. Pillco pleaded guilty to first-degree manslaughter and was sentenced to 25 years in prison without parole. He will be deported back to Ecuador when his sentence ends. Pillco ended up on a manslaughter rap because the authorities felt this was the safest way to ensure he got a conviction and a lengthy sentence. There is no doubt though that he murdered Adrienne Shelly.

Andy Ostroy later made a documentary in which he celebrated the life of his late wife. Their daughter (who tragically grew up without a mother), now a teenager, also worked on the documentary. It was a profoundly bittersweet experience making the documentary for both of them. Though they were happy and proud to celebrate Adrienne's life it was unavoidably also a sad experience. The most difficult part of the documentary for Ostroy was a scene in which he met the incarcerated Diego Pillco. The family of Adrienne Shelly set up a foundation in her memory. Though sadly gone, her legacy lives on.

In 1969, Sharon Tate was an actress who had appeared in films like The Fearless Vampire Killers and Valley of the Dolls. Her TV roles had included The Man from U.N.C.L.E. and The

Beverly Hillbillies. Her career was obviously boosted by the fact she was now married to the famous film director Roman Polanski. At 26 years of age, Sharon Tate seemed destined to become a huge star. Alas though, fate was to intervene in horrific fashion.

On August 8, 1969, Sharon Tate, who was nine months pregnant, was entertaining some friends at her Hollywood home. Her husband Roman Polanski was away in London making a film. Tate and her friends were subject to one of the most evil and infamous home invasions in history thanks to the orders of the nutty but charismatic cult leader Charles Manson. Manson had sent four of his 'followers' - Linda Kasabian, Tex Watson, Susan Atkins, and Patricia "Katie" Krenwinkel - to go and murder Tate. Tate's friends Jay Sebring, Wojciech Frykowski, and Abigail Folger, who were unfortunate enough to be in the house that night, were also killed.

The Manson cult members had cut the phone lines before they climbed over the walls to the property. Sharon Tate was stabbed nearly twenty times and had one of her breasts cut off. There were stab wounds from her head to her feet. The word 'pig' was scrawled on a door in her blood. This was a horrific attack on innocent people. The victims were beaten, hung, stabbed, shot, and suffered a dreadful ordeal. Charles Manson and three of the assailants were all sentenced to life in prison for this senseless and tragic act. Manson wasn't actually present at the murders but he had issued the instructions and egged on his brainwashed followers to commit these crimes.

Surprisingly, there seems to be no clear consensus of the type of person who will join a cult. Statistics indicate that very few cult members suffer from major psychological problems. Most cult members are just ordinary people. The reason for this is that cults like to have productive, functioning members who are good at recruiting others or making money for the cult. It doesn't do much good for a cult group if they only recruit dysfunctional people. Cults generally prefer to recruit intelligent well adjusted people. The more destructive cults will then use brainwashing and 'thought reform' on those they have recruited.

Away from his nutty cult group there was literally no one who didn't want Manson locked up for life and that's exactly what happened. Linda Kasabian escaped charges though because she didn't enter the house and was an eyewitness for the prosecution. The murders cast a dark cloud over Hollywood. As you might imagine, celebrities greatly increased their security. They hired guard dogs, got bigger gates, and employed private security guards. Many celebrities purchased guns lest they should face something similar.

After he returned from London, Roman Polanski had to be heavily sedated and ended up staying with the film producer Robert Evans. Evans was a friend of Polanski and Sharon Tate and could easily have been at the house that night. He was lucky he wasn't because he would have been murdered. The British actress Joanna Pettet visited Sharon Tate at the house that fateful day and left only hours before the home invasion took place. Talk about a lucky escape!

Manson's plan was to commit horrific crimes to blame on black Americans to incite a race war. This was a plan he named Helter Skelter. Needless to say, Manson was completely crazy. The author Joan Didion wrote of the Sharon Tate murders - "Many people I know in Los Angeles believe that the Sixties ended abruptly on August 9, 1969, ended at the exact moment when word of the murders on Cielo Drive travelled like brushfire through the community, and in a sense this is true." The murder of Sharon Tate was one of the most brutal and shocking in Hollywood history.

American Football legend OJ Simpson seemed to have the perfect life after he retired from sports. He had wealthy friends, lived in a beautiful house, was sought after for commercials and endorsements, and even began a successful acting career which saw him in appear in films like Capricorn

One and The Naked Gun. He had also developed business interests which maintained a regular flow of money and enabled him to live and move in swanky social circles.

But behind the scenes, Simpson was not the role model he was made out to be. His wife Nicole Brown Simpson was terrified of him and the police were regular visitors to their home because of domestic disturbances. Simpson though, who naturally knew all the police officers personally, could usually be relied on to smooth over any trouble with his personal charm and celebrity status. In 1995, Simpson was charged with the 1994 murders of his ex-wife Nicole Brown Simpson and her friend Ron Goldman - who had been stabbed multiple times.

An autopsy determined that Brown had been stabbed seven times in the neck and scalp, and had a 5.5 inches long gash across her throat, which had severed both her left and right carotid arteries and breached her right and left jugular veins. The wound on Brown's neck was so severe it had penetrated a depth of .75 inches into her cervical vertebrae, nearly decapitating her. She also had 'defensive' wounds on her hands. These were brutal murders of the type that serial killer would do. OJ Simpson was obviously the prime suspect - especially after the infamous Bronco chase. The police also knew he had a violent temper.

The case against OJ Simpson seemed fairly clear cut. Blood from the deceased was found in his car. A bloodied glove was also found on his property. Simpson had a motive too as he was prone to anger and jealousy whenever his wife became estranged from him. Remarkably though, and aided by the racial tensions in Los Angeles at the time because of the Rodney King affair, Simpson's street smart defence team of Johnnie Cochran, Robert Kardashian, and Robert Shapiro somehow managed to get Simpson a not guilty verdict. In the wake of the Rodney King incident, there were fears that if OJ was found guilty riots might erupt. This was a possible factor in the verdict. Nonetheless, many were astonished when he was found not guilty.

Cochran and Simpson's legal team made the trial about race. It was their forensic targeting of Police Detective Mark Fuhrman (the man who found much of the evidence that linked Simpson to the crimes) as much as anything that swayed the jury. They discovered that Fuhrman had once openly used racist language in an interview despite denying he hadn't. So, Fuhrman's testimony retrospectively became suspect and the police case against OJ was portrayed by the defense as a racist stitch-up. It didn't help that the police had not handled the case with the professional competence one might expect, especially when it came to collecting DNA and blood samples.

Simpson returned to his exclusive residence after the trial and resumed playing golf. He tried to get back to his normal life but this proved impossible. He was now a diminished and tainted figure. Many thought he was a murderer. The families of the victims filed a civil suit against him, and in 1997 a civil court awarded a $33.5 million judgement against Simpson for the victims' wrongful deaths. Simpson moved to Florida - a state where a person's residence cannot be seized to collect a debt under most circumstances. Most of his memorabilia was sold and his old friends had abandoned him.

Simpson became a semi-tragic character, doing trashy TV shows (like a Candid Camera clone) and womanising and drinking. OJ wrote a book called If I Did It and even pretended to stab Ruby Wax in a strange documentary about him. In September 2007, a group of men led by Simpson entered a room at the Palace Station hotel-casino and took sports memorabilia at gunpoint, which resulted in Simpson being questioned by police.

In 2008, he was convicted and sentenced to 33 years imprisonment, with a minimum of nine years without parole. It was a fittingly bizarre end to the OJ Simpson story. This was a ludicrously harsh punishment for the sports memorabillia incident and many saw the sentence as retrospective revenge for the murder charges that Simpson had avoided a decade before. Though he is now free, OJ Simpson remains a tarnished and strange figure - light years away from the man who was once so admired and loved.

In 1968, Albert Dekker was a veteran and much respected 62 year-old actor actor who had recently appeared in Bonanza and The Wild Bunch. Dekker had been appearing on the screen since 1937 and was a suave and distinguished looking man whose roles included East of Eden (with James Dean), the sci-fi horror film Dr. Cyclops, and the film noirs Kiss Me deadly and When Killers. When he went missing for a few days and failed to turn up to some appointments, Dekker's worried fiancée Jeraldine Saunders (who, to take a slight detour for the purposes of gratuitous trivia, created the TV show Love Boat) had his apartment door unlocked and found a very strange and unpleasant surprise.

Albert Dekker was dead in his bathtub and dressed in bondage gear with a noose around his neck. There were leather straps around his chest and rope binding his ankles. He had a ball gag in his mouth with pieces of metal chain tied round his head. His skin (including his buttocks) had obscene lipstick graffiti scrawled on it and there were hypodermic needles sticking out of him in various places. A vagina had been crudely drawn on his stomach. Jeraldine Saunders said that this grim and grisly scene haunted her for the rest of her life. It must have been a terrible and awful shock.

The official verdict was on Albert Dekker's death was accidental asphyxiation while attempting autoerotic asphyxia. However, there is a lot of dispute about this and many at the time believed that verdict was preposterous. Many believed this was a simple case of robbery and murder. Money ($70,000 in cash - a very sizeable sum in 1968) and camera equipment was missing and it seemed unlikely that Dekker could have written all over his body himself. How could he have scrawled on his own buttocks with lipstick? It wasn't impossible but given the amount of graffiti and the elaborate nature of the bondage gear it seemed questionable that he could have done all of this alone.

Jeraldine Saunders was convinced that Dekker was murdered and his friends never believed the bondage autoerotic asphyxia theory either because they thought it was completely out of character. Paul Lukas, a fellow actor and friend of Dekker, said - "Al never would leave the world in such a terrible shambles. He was a man of culture and breeding."

Believe it or not, the police originally (and preposterously) ruled Dekker's death as suicide. That would be a rather convoluted and strange way for someone to commit suicide! If he had decided to commit suicide then why did Dekker leave himself in such an embarrassing and strange situation for someone to find? That didn't make any sense.

It is believed that the police found S&M toys and porn in Dekker's apartment - which may have been a factor in leading them to the autoerotic asphyxia theory. There was no sign of forced entry in Dekker's apartment - which obviously must have been a factor in the police not ruling this a case of violent robbery. Jeraldine Saunders (who died in 2019 at the age of 95) believed though that the missing money and camera equipment meant it must have been a robbery which then turned into murder. Her theory was that the assailant must have been someone that Dekker knew and willingly let into the apartment. Dekker's son Benjamin had his own theory. He believed that Albert's death probably came as a result of a sex game gone wrong with a secret lover - who was presumably male. The secret lover must have fled the scene after helping himself to money and valuables.

Jenny Maxwell was born in New York in 1941. Blonde and cute, Maxwell was a hip and in demand actress in the late 50s and 1960s. Maxwell was friends with the doomed Sharon Tate and said to like the party life. She appeared in big television shows like The Twilight Zone and Bonanza and with Elvis in Blue Hawaii. Maxwell was also in the 1963 film Take Her,

She's Mine with Jimmy Stewart.

By the mid 1960s, Maxwell's star seemed to be on the wane. She had got divorced and lost custody of her son. She was broke and her career choices had become somewhat eccentric (she appeared in a strange film called Shotgun Wedding which was written by no lesser figure than Ed Wood). Her last acting credit was a 1968 appearance in the television show The Wild Wild West. Jenny evidently just seemed to lose interest in acting. Maybe the phone just stopped ringing and she couldn't be bothered with it anymore.

In 1970, Jenny Maxwell married Ervin M. Roeder. Roeder was a lawyer and twenty years older than Jenny. It has been suggested that Jenny married Roeder because she wanted some security and stability in her life now that her acting career was history. Ervin was pretty rich so she wouldn't have to worry about money so long as he was her husband. Roeder had connections in Hollywood and was said to be something of a blowhard who liked to give the impression he had mob connections.

The marriage between Maxwell and Roeder became very tense in the end. They both had affairs and Roeder was said to have become increasingly bitter at the thought of Jenny Jenny Maxwell inheriting all of his money should he shuffle off this mortal coil before her (which seemed more than likely given that she was much younger than him). Maxwell is alleged to have wanted to leave Roeder but clung onto the marriage because her lawyer told her that she would get a bigger divorce settlement if she was married past ten years.

On June the 10th, 1981, the couple were together in Beverly Hills because Roeder had offered Jenny a lift home after she visited a hospital for minor treatment. By now they were not living together but still on fairly civil terms. In the lobby of Maxwell's Beverly Hills condo that afternoon they were both shot and killed. Jenny was shot in the head while Roeder was shot in the abdomen. It was a puzzling double murder which was never officially solved. Jenny Maxwell was 39 years-old when her life came to this gruesome and sudden end. It was a mystery to the police why anyone would want to kill a former actress and her lawyer husband.

Years later a theory on the murder surfaced. The theory alleges that Roeder hired a hitman to kill Jenny that afternoon so he wouldn't have to pay spousal support. The hitman was, according to his theory, told to make it look real and so fire a shot at Roeder too or maybe give him a non lethal injury. The hitman, if this theory is true, was obviously not a very good shot! The hitman ended up killing the person who had hired him to kill his wife!

A weird detail in this case is that because Jenny was killed first in the lobby her estate legally transferred to her husband. When he died straight after, Roeder's children became the heirs to Jenny's estate. Jenny's son from her first marriage didn't get a penny. I'd imagine Jenny's son was quite bitter about that. I know I would be. Jenny Maxwell was later cremated and her ashes scattered at sea.

Christa Helm was born Sandra Lynn Wohlfeil on November the 11th, 1949 in Milwaukee, Wisconsin. Helm was a bit part actress. Her roles included a small part in the TV show Wonder Woman. She was also in the 1974 horror film Legacy of Satan. Christina apparently had quite a tough childhood and suffered some abuse from the men who lived with her mother. She got pregnant when she was sixteen but the father (who was ten years older) didn't bother to stick around and accept any responsibility. Helm worked as a waitress in various places to make ends meet and nearly became a Playboy bunny at one point. A chance meeting with the singer and actor James Darren made her decide she wanted to be an actress. This ambition was modestly facilitated when she met costume designer Linny Barron.

Barron helped introduce Christa to some 'movers and shakers' and through a producer she started getting a few acting bit

parts. Christa was the star of the 1974 low-budget action film
Let's Go for Broke. This film didn't do much business though.
Christa was dismayed when it didn't get a wide theatrical
release. She inevitably moved to Los Angeles in the end and
started living with a fiancer named Bernard Cornfeld in a
plush mansion. Christa was, to put it mildly, known as a party
girl. She would sleep with anyone - especially if she thought it
might help her career. It is said that when she a waitress other
waitresses used to warn her about taking home men she knew
nothing about but Christa never paid much attention. Christa
became notorious in Hollywood for her sexual exploits. Her
conquests included many famous people - including Warren
Beatty, Jack Nicholson, and Mick Jagger.

Christa apparently kept a diary which detailed all of her sexual
encounters with the rich and famous. She considered this
diary to be like a sort of pension or life insurance. It would
make a juicy memoir or lucrative newspaper article one day.
Christa is also alleged to have filmed some of her sexual
encounters with the rich and famous just to make sure she had
proof. There was later speculation had Christa plans to
blackmail Hollywood bigwigs with her diaries and movies. Her
friends are said to have warned her about speaking openly
about this diary. They thought she was playing a dangerous
game and would best advised to keep her mouth shut.

Despite all the Hollywood bed-hopping, Christa's career was
still in no danger of taking off. She still hardly had any acting
credits to her name. Her bit parts included a part as
(appropriately enough) a waitress in Starsky & Hutch.
Realising that her acting career had stalled and was going
nowhere fast, Christa made plans to record a disco album but
nothing much came of this either. It is said that she kept trying
to sleep with her female backing singers. She was very
ambitious and desperate to be famous but couldn't seem to
find an outlet or opening for a career in Hollywood.

In 1976, Christa is said to have dated the permanently tanned
and always dapper actor George Hamilton. She was also said

to be involved with the disc jockey Frankie Crocker. Christa was also linked to actors and producers. She evidently still had hopes that her acting career might yet get a boost from one of these connections. For a time, Christa lived in a loft with a woman named Patty Collins. They were also lovers but those who knew Christa later said they felt that Patty was trouble. They detected a tension between the two women and said that Christa planned to end the friendship.

On the night of February the 12th, 1977, Christa went to a Hollywood party in Laurel Canyon with her roommate Stephanie. At some point, Christa left the party. She was later found stabbed to death outside of her agent Sandy Smith's house. She was 27 years-old (there's that old curse again - a LOT of famous people, if one could call Christa famous, have died at the age of 27). Christa was stabbed 23 times and also beaten with a heavy object. Sandy Smith was allegedly asleep and heard nothing. Christa's blood splattered body was found by a young man who walked through that street shortly after the murder.

The tyre marks and abrupt fashion in which Christa's car was parked that night led police to suspect that someone was following her and she was trying to get to Smith's house for safety. Residents of the street told police they heard what sounded like an argument coming from outside and then a scream. The knife which carried out the murder was never found. In fact, the case was never solved at all.

There wasn't much media coverage of Christa's murder at all. She wasn't famous enough to warrant much ink. As for suspects, well, they certainly exist. The agent Sandy Smith was later found to be telling an untruth when he said he was asleep as Christa was being stabbed outside his house. He actually had guests that night. What was he trying to hide by this lie? Those who knew Christa thought the prime suspect was her old flame Patsy Collins - who was a backup singer and lover to Christa.

The story goes that Patsy was furious when Christa went cool on her and said she wasn't even gay anyway. Patsy, according to this theory, stabbed Christa to death in revenge. Another suspect is Rudy Mozella - who was a keyboard player in Christa's disco band. She was hoarding some cocaine for him. The theory in this instance is that Christa used some of the cocaine herself and he murdered her as a consequence. Believe it or not, one of the people interviewed by the police in relation to this murder was Tony Sirico - who later became famous playing Paulie Walnuts in The Sopranos. Sirico was one of the last people to visit Christa before her death.

Christa's diary and tapes detailing her sexual encounters went missing after her death. This has obviously led to speculation that she was killed by some Hollywood figure who feared that she might release embarrassing scandalous information about him. The main suspect though is still generally judged to have been Patsy Collins. One of the main reasons for this is not just their storied history together but also because Patsy suspiciously vanished after the murder.

The police never spoke to Patsy Collins about this murder because they had had no idea where she was. Modern forensic testing on this case has suggested that Christa had female DNA under her nails when she died. This would obviously tally with the Patsy Collins theory. Christa's daughter Nicole continues to work towards some sort of belated resolution in this case. She hasn't given up trying to solve the riddle of her mother's awful murder.

Lana Clarkson was born in Long Beach, California in 1962. She was a fashion model and actress. Clarkson was best known for B-movie roles but she had a number of small or background roles in mainstream movies like Fast Times at Ridgemont High, Brainstorm, and My Favorite Year. She also appeared in popular TV shows like Knight Rider, Three's Company, and The A-Team. Clarkson also appeared in five Roger Corman movies. You could probably describe Lana as a B-list star when it came to films. As a model though she went all over the world for photoshoots and was very successful.

Because her stock in trade was to play young pin-up type blondes, Clarkson found that her acting work began to dry up somewhat as she neared her forties. There was an endless assembly line of magazine model blondes in Hollywood so Clarkson eventually found the phone no longer rang as often as it used to. The sort of 'eye candy' background parts that she used to get in mainstream TV shows and movies were now being snapped up by younger women.

Ageism is a common complaint in Hollywood but it only seems to apply to women. Men can lead movies and get big paydays into their fifties and sixties but it's different for women. Geena Davis said that when turned forty it was like 'falling off a cliff'. Her phone suddenly stopped ringing. John Cusack said in an interview that he has actress friends who stopped getting work in their late twenties because by the youth obsessed standards of Hollywood they were already considered old!

By 2003, Lana Clarkson was working as a hostess at the House of Blues in West Hollywood, California. This job was necessary to pay the bills because the acting work was no longer as reliable as it used to be. Lana was living in fairly modest circumstances in a small house and had taken to selling photographs (presumably to B-movie fans) of herself online to make ends meet. At one point she even worked as a children's entertainer to bring in some extra cash. Lana was a good person by all accounts. She did voluntary work for an AIDS charity and always seemed cheerful and kind to people who met her.

On Sunday, February the 2nd, 2003, in what can only be described as a very cruel twist of fate, the shambling music legend Phil Spector arrived at the House of Blues sometime after midnight. Spector ambled into the club wearing one of his ridiculous toupees. Lana Clarkson actually refused him entry at first because she had no idea who he was. Spector had clearly been drinking - which was a bit worrying because he was supposed to be on the wagon. Spector was with another woman that night but she eventually left - leaving him alone. At this point he started chatting to Lana Clarkson - who by now had been informed by other staff members that this diminutive and toupeed character was very famous indeed.

Spector ordered champagne and evidently established a rapport with Clarkson because when her shift ended they left together and went back to his mansion. That would turn out to be the last shift Lana Clarkson ever worked in her life. It was around 2-30 am when they departed from the House of Blues. They are believed to have arrived at Spector's home about 3-30 am. What happened next was something that took two court trials to explain - and even then an element of mystery still remains. It was just a very weird case.

At five-thirty in the morning, after Lana had gone home with the music icon, Spector emerged from his house carrying a gun and told his limo driver - "I think I just shot her." Spector proved to be tragically accurate with this observation. He had indeed just shot poor Lana Clarkson. Lana was found dead in a chair. She had obviously been shot in the face and head. Her teeth were scattered all around and blood was very evident in the room. Spector was arrested by the police and then released on bail.

There were two trials in the end. The first was judged a mistrial because two members of the jury did not find Spector guilty of murder. They obviously needed a 100% unanimous verdict to convict. The second trial saw the 69 year-old Spector convicted for murder in the second degree. He was sentenced to nineteen years in prison and died in 2021 while still behind bars. Spector cut an eccentric figure in court to say the least. He wore a succession of increasingly bizarre wigs and frequently fired his defence team - not that it made any difference to the eventual outcome.

Spector's defence was that Clarkson had committed 'accidental' suicide by putting the gun in her mouth. Spector argued it was all an accident and not his fault. This claim was clearly not terribly convincing. It transpired in court that Spector had a history of pointing guns at women. It also transpired that his judgement was probably impaired by a head injury he received in the 1970s. Given the fact that the volatile and clearly bonkers Spector was prone to waving guns around and also off the wagon it was probably inevitable that something awful was going to happen in the end. What sort of person takes a woman back to their house and pulls a gun out?

In February 2012, Donna Clarkson, the mother of Lana, settled a civil lawsuit with Spector and his insurance company over the wrongful death of Lana Clarkson. Lana was laid to rest at Beth Olam Cemetery in Los Angeles. Spector lived on for eighteen years after Lana's death. All of this time was spent in prison. When he died he was described by one news outlet as talented but flawed. You could probably describe that morally dubious comment as the understatement of the century.

Barbara Colby was an American actress known for her comedic flair and toothy smile. As a young woman she studied acting (which included a spell in Paris) and then won plaudits for her work in the theatre. She made her Broadwy debut in 1965. Her first major television break came in a 1971 episode of Columbo and she went on to appear in a number of television shows which included The Odd Couple, Gunsmoke, and Kung Fu. In 1975, Colby played a prostitute named Sherry Ferris in two episodes of The Mary Tyler Moore Show. Colby was a very good scene stealer and had good comic timing.

Barbara Colby's career seemed to be starting to take off by this point and it didn't seem far-fetched to think that she might soon have her own sitcom or start to pick up parts in movies. Colby was married twice and had homes in New York and Malibu. She had a pretty good life. Colby was into Vedanta and spirituality. This kept her grounded and down to earth. She also loved psychics and tarot readings. She believed in karma and reincarnation.

On July 24, 1975, Barbara Colby was on her way home after teaching an acting class in Venice, CA. She was with a colleague named James Kiernan. As was their custom, they stopped the car in a parking lot and took a break from the long drive. Apparently, this was a tradition for Colby. She liked to take a break and talk about acting with whoever was with her on the way home. While Colby and her friend chatted, a van approached containing two men. The men shot Colby and Kiernan once and then drove away. It was a random and senseless drive by shooting. The shooters didn't even attempt to rob the victims. One of the bullets had hit Colby in the chest and damaged her lung. She almost instantly died of the injuries. She was only 36 years-old.

Kiernan was taken to hospital and managed to give a description of the shooters to the police before he too died of his injuries. Despite the police having a description of the shooters the murders were never solved and no one was convicted for the deaths of Colby and Kiernan. Some men were arrested but it transpired they had nothing to do with the deaths and so they were set free. It appears that the murders were completely random. The men in question didn't even know they were killing a celebrity.

At the time there was a huge spike in these sorts of incidents in Los Angeles with homicides and drive by shootings going through the roof. Colby was just desperately unlucky to be in the wrong place at the wrong time. She shoudn't have stopped in that part of town but then hindsight is a wonderful thing. Colby obviously had no way of knowing that stopping for a break in a car parking lot was going to come at the cost of her life.

Barbara Colby's last role was in a 1976 television movie called The Ashes of Mrs. Reasoner in which she starred with Charles During. Colby was murdered three weeks before this movie aired on television. Colby was cremated and her ashes were scattered in the Pacific Ocean. Celebrities and co-stars like Mary Tyler Moore, Cloris, Ed Asner, and Cloris Leachman

attended the funeral service. At the time of her death, Colby
was playing Liz Erskine in the sitcom Phyllis - which was a sort
of spin-off from The Mary Tyler Moore Show. Liz Torres took
over the role after Barbara Colby's sad death.

Dorothy Stratten was an actress, model and Playboy playmate.
She appeared in Buck Rogers in the 25th Century, Fantasy
Island, and the bargain basement but cultish sci-fi film
Galaxina. She also got a small part in the Peter Bogdanovich
film They All Laughed. Bogdanovich fell in love with Stratten
and they began an affair. The only problem was that Stratten
was married to a pimp and hustler named Paul Snider.
Stratten wanted to start a new life with Bogdanovich and so
arranged to meet Snider (from whom she was estranged) to
ask for a divorce. Stratten was advised by Bogdanovich and
Hugh Hefner not to go and meet Snider but she did so anyway.

Dorothy Stratten met Snider in the home they used to share
and it would tragically be the last night of their life. Snider
turned up with a shotgun and killed Stratten by shooting her
in the face. She was only twenty years-old. Snider then shot
himself. Stratten had also been raped by some sort of bizarre
bondage contraption that Snider had set up. The authorities
were never able to establish though if Stratten had been alive
or dead when she was sexually assaulted. Bogdanovich was
devastated by Stratten's death. Several years later he raised a
few eyebrows by marrying Dorothy's younger sister Louise
(who was only twelve when Bogdanovich first met her). The
marriage lasted until 2001. Two films were made based on this
sad case in the wake of Dorothy Stratten's death - Death of a
Centerfold: The Dorothy Stratten Story and Star 80 starring
Mariel Hemingway.